Seaplanes

& Flying Boats

Zooming over the NORTH ATLANTIC erasing barriers of time and space...a **CONSOLIDATED FLYING BOAT** charts new paths for AMERICAN EXPORT AIRLINES

Seaplanes
& Flying Boats

**A TIMELESS COLLECTION
FROM AVIATION'S GOLDEN AGE**

Bill Yenne

with illustrations by John Batchelor

BCL Press
New York

Published by BCL Press/Book Creation, LLC, by arrangement with O.G. Publishing, Corp.

2003 BCL Press/Book Creation, LLC

Text © 1997 Bill Yenne. Design © 1997 American Graphic Systems, Inc.

Designed and captioned by Bill Yenne, with design assistance by Azia Yenne.
Proofreading and indexing by Andy Roe.

Page one photograph: A 1939 advertisement for the Consolidated Catalina expressing the optimistic promise of seaplane travel.
Page two photograph: A close-up view of a PBY in World War II warpaint shows its smooth 1930s styling.
Photo above: The *Indian Ocean Tradewind*, a Convair R3Y-2, taxis into Honolulu harbor with Diamond Head visible in the distance.

M 10 9 8 7 6 5 4 3 2 1

ISBN 1-932302-03-4

Printed in China

TABLE OF CONTENTS

INTRODUCTION 6

THE GLENN CURTISS HYDROPLANES 10

THE BOEING FLOATPLANES 12

THE SHORT FLOATPLANES 14

THE MARTIN FLOATPLANES 16

THE CURTISS HS FLYING BOATS 18

THE BOEING B-1 FLYING BOAT 20

EARLY SAVOIA FLYING BOATS 22

THE MARTIN PM-1 24

THE MARTIN MS-1 26

THE CONSOLIDATED XPY-1 ADMIRAL 28

THE CONSOLIDATED COMMODORE 30

THE MARTIN P3M AND XP2M 32

THE MACCHI FLYING BOATS 34

THE VOUGHT O2U CORSAIR 36

SEAPLANES FOR THE SCHNEIDER RACE 38

THE DORNIER DO.X 44

THE DORNIER WAL 46

THE DOUGLAS XO2D 48

THE LATÉCOÈRE FLYING BOATS 52

THE CONSOLIDATED P2Y RANGER 54

THE SAVOIA MARCHETTI S.55 58

THE SIKORSKY S-38 62

THE SHORT EMPIRE FLYING BOATS 64

THE SHORT/MAYO COMPOSITE 66

THE DOUGLAS DOLPHIN 68

THE SIKORSKY S-42 CLIPPER 72

THE LOCKHEED SIRIUS *TINGMISSARTOQ* 74

THE SUPERMARINE WALRUS 76

THE CURTISS CONDOR 78

THE MARTIN M-130 CLIPPER 80

THE BOEING 314 CLIPPER 84

THE HEINKEL HE.115 90

THE CONSOLIDATED PBY CATALINA 92

THE CONSOLIDATED PB2Y CORONADO 100

THE ARADO AR.196 102

THE DORNIER DO.24 104

THE DORNIER DO.26 108

THE BLOHM UND VOSS BV.138 112

THE GRUMMAN DUCK 114

THE KAWANISHI H8K 116

THE SHORT S.25 SUNDERLAND 118

THE SHORT S.25V SANDRINGHAM 122

THE MARTIN MARS 124

THE VOUGHT OS2U KINGFISHER 128

THE BLOHM UND VOSS BV.222 WIKING 130

THE MARTIN PBM MARINER 134

THE MARTIN P5M MARLIN 138

THE MARTIN P6M SEAMASTER 140

THE CONVAIR P5Y/R3Y TRADEWIND 144

THE HUGHES HK-1 "SPRUCE GOOSE" 148

THE CONVAIR SEADART 150

THE GRUMMAN GOOSE 152

THE GRUMMAN WIDGEON 154

THE GRUMMAN MALLARD 156

RECENT DORNIER SEAPLANES 158

THE DEHAVILLAND BEAVER 160

THE GRUMMAN ALBATROSS 162

THE SHIN MEIWA PS-1 166

THE CANADAIR CL-215 168

THE CANADAIR CL-415 170

INDEX 174

Seaplanes hold a special place in our memory of the wonderful aircraft of aviation's golden age. Streamlined by necessity, they were magnificent and beautiful machines that caught and held the eye and the imagination. Contributions to aviation history aside, the gleaming wood or metal hulls and art deco styling of the great flying boats made them enduring masterpieces of design and applied arts.

Henri Fabre was not the first to imagine lifting from the water into the air in a powered vehicle, but at Lac Berre, near Martigues in southern France in March 1908, he became the first man to live the dream. The notion of building and flying "hydroplanes," as they were then known, was quickly embraced by Glenn Curtiss in upstate New York, where he produced many of the most important early seaplanes.

The golden age of seaplanes commenced in the 1920s, as seaplanes gave early airline entrepreneurs an opportunity to provide scheduled air service to areas without airfields. Soon, the notion that "every lake is an airport" became a popular marketing tool.

Beginning with Curtiss, this book surveys that golden age and the great moments in seaplane history, from the early floatplanes through the great Supermarine and Macchi racers of the Schneider Cup era, to the great Pan American Clippers of the 1930s.

To begin this overview, we should perhaps ask ourselves the question: "What is a seaplane?" The answer is simply "any airplane that operates from the surface of the water rather than the land."

There are many types of seaplanes, although that term was originally coined to apply only to the type of aircraft which we now refer to as "floatplanes." A floatplane is an aircraft with a conventional landplane fuselage that is situated on pontoons rather than on wheels. In fact, many floatplane types, such as the de Havilland Beaver, have also been produced in a landplane variation.

A second type of seaplane is the "flying boat." These aircraft differ from floatplanes in that their fuselage itself sits in the water rather than being positioned above it on a pontoon. The flying boat takes its name from the fact that its fuselage is really a boat-like hull. In fact, nautical terms generally apply to flying boats, whose fuselages are referred to as their hulls, whose noses as bows, and so on.

The halcyon era of flying boats came in the years between the World Wars, when air travel was increasingly popular, but when many airports were not yet large enough to handle aircraft with large passenger loads. With seaplanes, runway length is determined only by the length of the lake, bay or river at hand.

RIGHT: THE POPULAR ITALIAN
PIAGGIO P.166 TURBOPROP SEA-
PLANE. *BELOW:* THE BEECH 18 WAS
NOT DESIGNED AS A SEAPLANE, BUT
MANY HAVE BEEN RETROFITTED IN
FLOATPLANE CONFIGURATION.
OPPOSITE BOTTOM: PART ON A
LONG LINE OF SOVIET FLYING
BOATS, THE BERIEV A40
ALBATROSS TURBO-FANJET-POW-
ERED FLYING BOAT FIRST FLEW IN
1986 AND ENTERED SOVIET AIR
FORCE SERVICE IN 1988.

In the 1920s and 1930s, scheduled air service across the Atlantic — and later across the Pacific — was pioneered by the great flying boats of many nations. Germany's Dornier, Italy's Savoia Marchetti, and Britain's Short Brothers all produced milestone aircraft during this period.

As with the class of animals of the same name, an "amphibian" is a seaplane — either a floatplane or a flying boat — which is equally at home on land or water. Just as animal amphibians have gills as well as lungs, amphibious aircraft have hulls or pontoons in addition to landing gear. While many non-amphibious seaplanes have small wheels, or "beaching gear," an amphibian has wheels that are fully capable of routine runway landings.

During World War II, seaplanes were an important part of the military arsenal of every major combatant. Flying boats served as long-range patrol bombers and transports, while floatplanes were standard equipment aboard battleships and cruisers. Floatplanes functioned as the eyes of the fleet. Another valuable service performed by seaplanes of all sizes and hull types was air-sea rescue. Numerous downed pilots and sunken ship survivors owed their lives to seaplanes and their daring crews.

When the war ended, however, the golden age of seaplanes ceased as well. Helicopters replaced floatplanes as the eyes of the fleet and in many air-sea rescue operations. The great and luxurious flying boat airliners whose promising careers were interrupted by the war had now been supplanted by larger landplanes operating from much larger airports.

Today, though the golden age may be gone, it is not forgotten, nor are many important seaplane applications. The bush pilots of Alaska and northern Canada would be lost without their de Havilland Beavers and Cessna floatplanes. Japan's Shin Meiwa flying boats are still operating in maritime patrol missions for which nations such as Britain and the United States abandoned seaplanes long ago. Meanwhile, companies such as Canadair are producing new generations of flying boats as water-scoopers.

We invite you to join us in these pages for a celebration of these great historic aircraft, of their bygone golden age, and of a promising future for a new generation of seaplanes.

RIGHT: **A** BRACE OF **V**OUGHT **OS2U-3** **K**INGFISHERS TAXIING IN FORMATION. *BELOW:* **A PBY** **C**ATALINA OVER A FOGGY **C**ALIFORNIA COASTLINE. *OPPOSITE BOTTOM:* **B**UILT IN **1912**, THE **C**URTISS **C-1** WAS THE **US N**AVY'S FIRST BOAT-HULLED SEAPLANE.

THE GLENN CURTISS HYDROPLANES

Many young men — and women too — have an interest in machines and enjoy tinkering with them to understand how they work and how to make them work better. Some of these people grow up to spend their afternoons working on the family car, but others grow up to become engineers and inventors. The beginning of the twentieth century was an exciting time for young tinkers. The compact and practical internal combustion engine had been perfected, and was available to be applied to all sorts of exciting vehicles.

Wilbur and Orville Wright were part of this generation, and so was Glenn Hammond Curtiss, the man who can probably be credited with the first practical seaplane and the first practical flying boat. Born in Hammondsport in upstate New York in 1878, Curtiss started racing motorcycles in his teens and turned to building motorcycle engines. In 1901, he started building lightweight engines for Army dirigibles, and in 1907, he joined Alexander Graham Bell's Aerial Experiment Association (AEA), for which he became the star designer. In 1908, he designed the AEA's first aircraft, the *June Bug*. Later in 1908, the AEA produced its first seaplane, the *Loon*, which was essentially a variation on Curtiss' *June Bug* mounted on twin pontoons. Hammondsport was located on Lake Keuka, which would provide the "runway" for this and the family of seaplanes that Curtiss was to produce over the coming years.

It was in 1910 that Curtiss began building his "hydroplanes." Although Henri Fabre had been the first to fly a seaplane, it was Glenn Curtiss who was likely the first to fully exploit the notion of water-borne aircraft. The first Curtiss hydroplane was a variation on the Model D landplane.

Known as the Model D Hydro, it was constructed in San Diego, and made its first flight in January 1911. It was a biplane, 28 feet 8 inches in length and it had a wing span of 36 feet 11 inches, with ailerons on the top wing. The D Hydro was powered by a Curtiss Type O single-rocker V-8 engine, in a pusher configuration, which delivered 60 horsepower. It had a single float that was 7 feet 1 inch long and 6 feet 3 inches wide.

The D Hydro evolved into the Model D-III Tractor Hydro, which, of course, had its engine and propeller in a tractor configuration. This aircraft attracted the attention of the US Navy. In fact, when Curtiss completed his February 17, 1911 flight, he and the D-III were hoisted aboard the USS *Pennsylvania* for tea.

Returning to Hammondsport in 1912, Curtiss then developed the Model E, considered by some to have been the first successful flying boat. In 1914, Curtiss built the first twin-engine flying boat, the Model H. Eventually, Curtiss would build 124 of them for the US Navy in what is probably the first mass-production of a seaplane. Some were also exported to Britain, where the design formed the basis for the Felixtowe F.2.

The most famous Model H series boat was the *America*, constructed in 1914 for the purpose of being the first aircraft to fly the Atlantic Ocean. It was 38 feet in length and had a wing span of 74 feet, with the ailerons on the top wing. It was powered by a pair of Curtiss Type OX inline engines in pusher configuration, rated at 90 horsepower.

The flight, via Newfoundland and the Azores, was to have included two pilots, one from the US Navy, and one from the British Royal Navy. However, when the first world war began in August 1914, the flight was cancelled because of concerns over potential danger.

In May 1919, six months after the war ended, a Curtiss NC-4 flying boat would make the first successful air crossing of the Atlantic.

RIGHT: FLIGHT TESTED OFF SAN DIEGO'S NORTH ISLAND, THE CURTISS D HYDRO AND THE FOLLOW-ON MODEL E WERE PROBABLY THE WORLD'S FIRST PRACTICAL SEAPLANES. *BELOW:* GLENN CURTISS ABOARD THE MODEL H *AMERICA* DURING TAXI TESTS ON LAKE KEUKA, NEW YORK.

THE BOEING FLOATPLANES

The Boeing Airplane Company, which is today renown for being the world's largest producer of commercial aircraft, had its beginnings in 1916 as a producer of float-planes. When William Edward "Bill" Boeing founded the company in partnership with naval officer Conrad Westervelt, the idea was to compete with companies such as Curtiss' who were then producing seaplanes.

To facilitate launching their products after they were built, Boeing and Westervelt rented, as a factory, a small boathouse on the shore of Lake Union in the heart of Seattle. Their first aircraft, designated as the B&W after its creators, made its maiden flight from Lake Union on June 15, 1916. It was 27 feet 6 inches in length, and it had a wing span of 52 feet. It had a gross weight of 2,800 pounds. The B&W, also known as Boeing Model 1, was powered by a Hall-Scott A-5 engine rated at 125 horsepower. The aircraft had a cruising speed of 67 mph and a range of 320 miles.

While there were no domestic customers for the B&W, two were sold to the government of New Zealand, who used one to make the first airmail flight in that country.

After the B&W, Westervelt left the company, but Boeing proceeded with development of the Model C, a follow-on to the earlier aircraft. A pair of these aircraft were ordered by the US Navy, and the first one flew on November 15, 1916. When the United States entered World War I five months later, the Navy ordered another 50 aircraft and the US Army ordered two landplane versions.

The ultimate Model C was the C-5. It was 27 feet in length, and had a wing span of 43 feet 10 inches. It had a gross weight of 2,395 pounds. Powered by a Hall-Scott A-7A rated at 125 horsepower, the C-5 had a cruising speed of 65 mph, a service ceiling of 6,500 feet and a range of 200 miles.

All but one of those delivered to the US Navy had twin pontoons. This aircraft had one large center pontoon and a pair of small auxiliary floats under the wings. Designated as the C-1F, this aircraft was powered by a Curtiss OX-5 engine.

In addition to the US Navy orders, Boeing produced two landplane variants for the US Army, and one was also built for Bill Boeing's personal use. On March 3, 1919, Boeing and pioneer aviator Eddie Hubbard used this C-5 to make the first international airmail flight to the United States when they flew a bag of mail to Seattle from Vancouver, British Columbia.

RIGHT: THE B&W IS ROLLED DOWN THE RAMP INTO LAKE UNION IN PREPARATION FOR ITS FIRST FLIGHT ON JUNE 15, 1916. *BELOW:* ONE OF THE LATER BOEING C-5 FLOATPLANES IN THE LAKE UNION BOATHOUSE FACTORY. ONE SUCH AIRCRAFT WOULD MAKE AMERICA'S FIRST INTERNATIONAL AIRMAIL FLIGHT. *OPPOSITE BOTTOM:* BOEING AND WESTERVELT'S B&W PARKED ON LAKE UNION IN SEATTLE.

THE SHORT FLOATPLANES

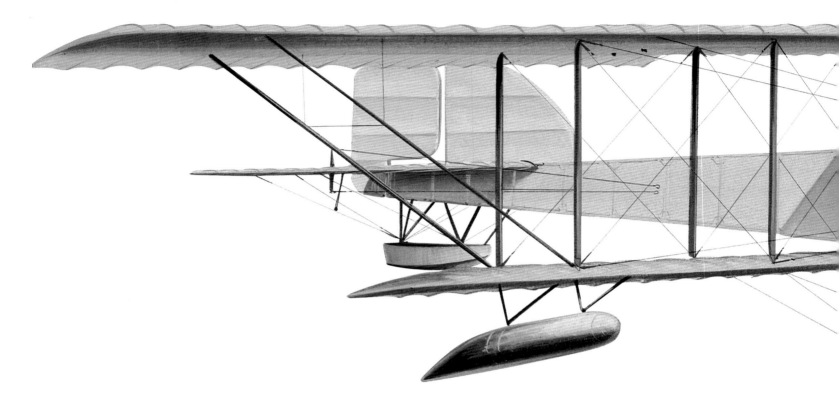

The Short brothers, Horace and Eustace, formed their aircraft company before World War I with an eye to developing aircraft that could be carried aboard British warships as reconnaissance vehicles. An important aspect of naval operations is being able to see beyond the horizon in order to be able to engage a potential enemy as soon as he is sighted. Because of the curvature of the Earth, the higher one is aboard a ship, the farther one can see. An airplane can naturally fly higher than the highest point on any ship. An airplane can also improve the accuracy of a warship's guns by helping the gunner triangulate distance. Finally, an aircraft can fly far from a ship to conduct reconnaissance missions.

These were all factors in the Short brothers being able to sell a series of floatplanes to the British Admiralty. The first was the Short 74, which entered service with His Majesty's Navy on the eve of World War I. Powered by a 100 horsepower Gnome engine, the 74 was succeeded by the Short 166, which was also known as "Folder."

The Short Folder took its name from its being constructed with folding wings, which had been patented by the Shorts in 1913. It was powered by a 200 horsepower Salmson engine, and was configured to carry a torpedo to augment its role as a reconnaissance aircraft.

The Short 166 evolved, in turn, into the Short 184, which had the distinction of being the first aircraft to operate successfully as an offensive weapon in a naval engagement. This took place on August 12, 1915, when Short floatplanes flying from the seaplane carrier HMS *Ben-My-Chree* sank a Turkish supply ship with a torpedo in the Sea

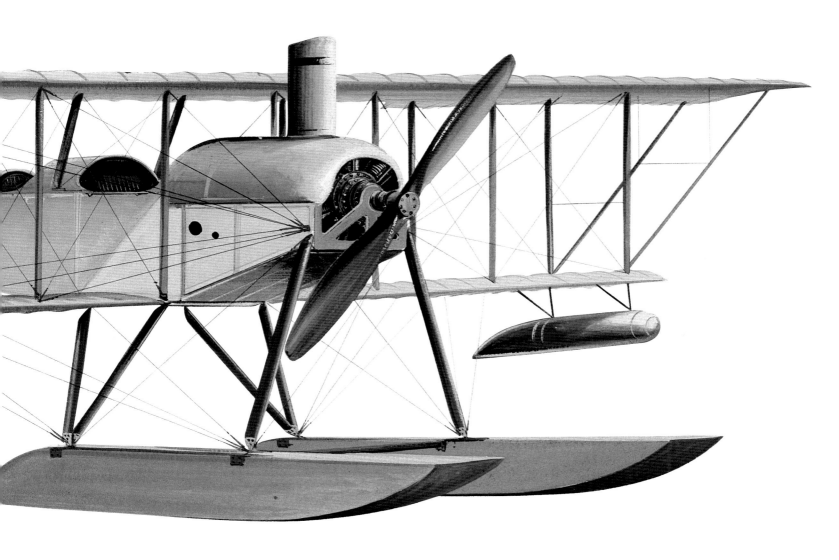

of Marmara during the Battle of Gallipoli. The twin-float Short seaplane was also used as a gun-spotting aircraft against the Germans during the Battle of Jutland, the key naval engagement of the first World War.

The Short 184 was 40 feet 7.5 inches in length, and had a wing span of 63 feet 6 inches. It had a gross weight of 5,560 pounds. Most of the more than 900 aircraft of this type that were built were powered by a single Sunbeam engine rated at 225 horsepower. However, several other engines were used during the production run. The aircraft had a maximum speed of 88 mph, and an endurance of 2 hours 45 minutes.

Both the Short 166 Folder and Short 184 were armed with a 14-inch-diameter torpedo and/or bombs in various configurations.

ABOVE: **THE SHORT BROTHERS 166 WAS KNOWN AS "FOLDER" BECAUSE OF ITS FOLDING WINGS. THIS WAS DONE TO PERMIT COMPACT STORAGE ABOARD BRITISH WARSHIPS.**

THE MARTIN FLOATPLANES

Glenn Luther Martin built his first pusher biplane in 1909 at the age of 23 and took up exhibition flying. By 1912, he had become the second person to earn the Aero Club of America's Expert Aviator Certificate. Martin earned this honor with a record 34-mile, 37-minute seaplane flight from Newport Bay on the California coast to Catalina Island on May 10.

He then formed the Glenn L. Martin Company to build airplanes, founded a flying school, and produced the first American-made multi-engine bomber for the US Army. Like Glenn Curtiss, Glenn Martin had an interest in seaplanes. His first was a military trainer, the Model TA Hydro of 1914, a four-seater with a large main float, plus wingtip and tail floats. The following year, he delivered his Model TT (for "tractor trainer") to the US Army.

The Martin Model R was a two-seat reconnaissance biplane, of which 27 were built by Martin in 1916 and Wright-Martin between 1916 and 1917. The Model R was powered by a Hall-Scott engine rated at 150 horsepower. This gave the aircraft a top speed of 86 mph at sea level. The seaplane version had twin-floats and rigid outer struts. On the eve of the American entry into World War I, Martin produced the Model S, a sister ship to the Model R.

After the war, the US Navy commissioned Martin to build the MO-1 (Martin, Observation, first), which could be catapult-launched from the stern of cruisers or battleships to extend their visual range. The ships typically carried a pair of seaplanes, and later ships had a pair of catapults which used compressed steam to launch the planes. The MO-1 had an all-metal framework, with the fuselage framed in welded steel and the wings in aluminum alloy. Wood was used in the engine mount to absorb vibration. A total of 36 MO-1s were delivered to the US Navy between April 1923 and January 1924.

RIGHT: US ARMY PERSONNEL PREPARE TO LAUNCH A MARTIN TT FLOATPLANE. BELOW: TWO MARTIN MO-1S ON THEIR CATAPULT ABOARD THE BATTLESHIP USS MISSISSIPPI, ANCHORED AT NORTH ISLAND IN SAN DIEGO HARBOR. THEY ARE SEEN HERE WITH WHEEL GEAR ATTACHED TO FLOATS. OPPOSITE BOTTOM: NAVY PERSONNEL IN WATER WITH MODEL S SEAPLANE NUMBER A69 IN 1917. NOTE THE GAP BETWEEN FUSELAGE AND LOWER WING.

THE CURTISS HS FLYING BOATS

The Curtiss HS series of flying boats were a natural evolution of the Model H series of flying boats that were born in the years before World War I and adapted by Felixstowe for production in the United Kingdom. This series included such important aircraft as the H-1 *America*, which was designed to fly the Atlantic Ocean.

The final Model H flying boats had been the twin-engine, pusher propeller H-16 aircraft that were being developed concurrently with the single-engine HS craft. The prototype HS-1L was delivered with a 200 horsepower Curtiss VXX engine, but production HS-2Ls had 400 horsepower Liberty 12 engines.

The HS-2L became the standard US Navy flying boat during World War I and was the only indigenously-designed US aircraft to serve in Europe during the war. The first recorded attack by an HS boat on a U-boat was on July 21, 1918 off Cape Cod, but the bomb was a dud. The U-156 skulked away to prey on Allied shipping in the North Atlantic.

The HS-2L carried a crew of three, was armed with a single machine gun, and had a 600-pound bomb load. It was 39 feet in length and had a wing span of 74 feet 1 inch. It had a gross weight of 6,432 pounds. The HS-2L's Liberty engine gave it a top speed of 85 mph, and it had a range of 575 miles.

There were a total of 673 HS-2Ls constructed, primarily between 1918 and the early months of 1919. In order to achieve the necessary level of production, Curtiss licensed Boeing, Gallaudet and Loughead (later Lockheed) to build nearly 100 of the aircraft.

The US Naval Aircraft Factory also built a total of 24 at Naval Air Stations such as Anacostia, Coco Solo, Hampton Roads, Key West, Miami and San Diego. These were produced using Curtiss-supplied parts.

The HS-3 was similar to the HS-2L, but had a redesigned hull. However, only six HS-3s were built before the project was cancelled.

THE BOEING B-1 FLYING BOAT

After World War I, many aircraft builders turned from military to civilian aircraft. With accommodations for two passengers plus the pilot, Boeing's B-1 was conceived with the many lakes, inlets and waterways of the Pacific Northwest in mind. The B-1 was 31 feet 3 inches in length and had a wing span of 50 feet 3 inches. It weighed 3,850 pounds fully loaded. The B-1 was designed to be powered by either a 200 horsepower Hall-Scott L-6 or a 400 horsepower Liberty engine. It had a top speed of 90 mph, a cruising speed of 80 mph, and a service ceiling of 13,300 feet. With a range of 400 miles, it was used on the Victoria to Seattle airmail route.

RIGHT: BUILDING THE B-1. BELOW: AVIATION PIONEER
EDDIE HUBBARD CHALKED UP 350,000 AIR MILES FROM
1920 TO 1928, WHILE FLYING AIRMAIL BETWEEN SEATTLE
AND VICTORIA, BRITISH COLUMBIA IN THIS AIRCRAFT.

EARLY SAVOIA FLYING BOATS

During the 1920s, Italy blossomed as an important center of seaplane development. Perhaps the best known Italian seaplane-maker of the era was Societa Idrovolanti Alta Italia, better known as Savoia. The most important among the first generation flying boats from Savoia was the S.16, which was introduced in 1919 as a military patrol plane. In 1921, a bomber version of the S.16 was produced, but it is best remembered as a commercial aircraft.

The S.16ter stood out as the most prominent S.16 variant. The most important S.16ter was the *Gennariello*, which was used for a remarkable endurance flight in 1925.

Piloted by Francesco de Pinedo, with Ernesto Campinelli as flight engineer, the *Gennariello* took off from Sesto Calende on Lake Maggiore on April 20, bound for Tokyo and Melbourne. They landed on the Tiber River in Rome on November 7, having covered a record-setting 35,000 miles in 360 flying hours.

The success of the 1925 record flight led to commercial sales for the S.16ter in 1926 and 1927. Aero Espresso adopted it, as did Societa Italiana Servizi Aerei, who used it on the route between San Remo and Genoa.

The S.16ter was 32 feet 5.75 inches in length, 12 feet high, and had a wing span of 50 feet 10.25 inches. It weighed 5,732 pounds and was powered by a 12-cylinder Lorraine-Dietrich liquid-cooled engine (license-built in Italy by Isotta-Fraschini) rated at 400 horsepower. This gave the trim Savoia a cruising speed of 93 mph, while its range was 620 miles. It had a service ceiling of 9,800 feet, although in 1924, it set a world flying boat altitude record of 15,081 feet.

Another Italian flying boat producer of note was Cantieri Cavali Triestini (CANT), which was already known as a producer of military aircraft when it began producing civilian flying boats in 1926. Their first was the Cant 6ter, a

large trimotor biplane that could accommodate 11 passengers. One of the vehicles was sold to Societa Italiana Servizi Aerei, but no other customers were forthcoming.

Meanwhile, however, Cantieri Cavali Triestini was working on the more compact four-passenger Cant 10ter, which was more readily accepted by the airlines. Societa Italiana Servizi Aerei began putting them into service as early as April 1926 on the route connecting Trieste and Turin, by way of Venice and Pavia.

The 10ter was quite similar in size to the Savoia S.16ter. Measuring 36 feet 7 inches in length and 13 feet 4 inches high, it had a wing span of 50 feet 2.5 inches and weighed 6,600 pounds. This Cant was powered by a 12-cylinder Lorraine-Dietrich engine (license-built in Italy by Isotta-Fraschini) rated at 400 horsepower. This gave the 10ter a cruising speed of 93 mph. It had a service ceiling of 13,700 feet, and its range was 370 miles.

ABOVE, BOTH: A TRACTOR VARIANT OF THE SOCIETA IDROVOLANTI ALTA ITALIA (SAVOIA) S.16, WHICH HAD A PUSHER PROPELLER DRIVEN BY A 12-CYLINDER LORRAINE-DIETRICH LIQUID-COOLED ENGINE (LICENSE-BUILT IN ITALY BY ISOTTA-FRASCHINI). THE RECORD-SETTING FLIGHT BY FRANCESCO DE PINEDO AND ERNESTO CAMPINELLI IN 1925 LED TO SALES OF SAVOIA FLYING BOATS IN ITALY AND AROUND THE WORLD.

THE MARTIN PM-1

During the first World War, the United States relied heavily on foreign-produced aircraft, although the US Navy had made good use of its Curtiss-designed HS series flying boats. When the United States entered the war in 1917, the Navy had only six flying boats, but on Armistice Day in 1918, the number had swelled to 1,172 — over half of them HS boats. With all of these vehicles on hand, there was little impetus to build more. The Navy would not produce flying boats in quantity for a decade, and many of those that were built came from the Naval Aircraft Factory.

When flying boat patrol bombers did return to the budget, one of the most notable was the Martin PM-1 — itself a variation on the Naval Aircraft Factory PN-12. The Martin seaplane was 49 feet 2 inches in length, 16 feet 4 inches high, and had a wing span of 72 feet 10 inches. Total wing area was 1,236 square feet. Empty, it weighed 8,970 pounds, and had a gross weight of 16,117 pounds.

The PM-1 was powered by a pair of Wright R-1820-64 Cyclone engines, each rated at 575 horsepower. This power gave it a top speed of 118 mph at sea level. The PM-1 had a service ceiling of 9,000 feet, and its range was 1,510 miles.

Martin delivered 27 PM-1s between July and October 1930. The following year, the company built 25 PM-2s, an upgraded version with twin rudders that was based on the Naval Aircraft Factory P4N.

The PM-2 was nearly identical to the PM-1 in size and appearance, but weighed 9,919 pounds empty, 17,284 pounds fully loaded. It was powered by the same R-1820-64 Cyclone engines. It had a service ceiling of 9,500 feet. Maximum range was 1,347 miles with no payload, or 937 miles with a full bomb load.

RIGHT: **A PM-2** OF PATROL SQUADRON **VP-2.** THE **PM-2** HAD TWIN TAILS AND MORE POWERFUL COWLED ENGINES. *BELOW:* **A PM-1** OVER **SAN DIEGO.** *OPPOSITE BOTTOM:* THE FIRST **PM-1** IS LAUNCHED FROM THE **MARTIN** RAMP AT **DARK HEAD COVE** DURING THE SUMMER OF 1930.

THE MARTIN MS-1

The Martin Model 63 was developed in 1923 as a unique innovation in the use of aircraft to extend the reach of warships. At a time when the US Navy was producing its first aircraft carrier, the USS *Langley* (CV-1), the idea evolved to build a small floatplane that could be carried aboard submarines.

The Model 63 was a naval scout airplane ordered by the US Navy under the designation MS-1 for Martin Submarine Observation. It was designed to fold up and be carried inside sealed tanks on the deck of submarines. Fully loaded, the MS-1 weighed only 1,000 pounds.

There were six MS-1s that had been ordered and completed when the program was cancelled in 1924. The concept was revived during World War II by the Japanese, who launched one air attack against Oregon using a submarine-launched aircraft.

After World War II, the US Navy adopted a similar concept. Submarines such as USS *Growler*, USS *Grayback* and USS *Halibut* were configured with water-tight hangars to carry the Vought Regulus SSM-N cruise missile — actually an unmanned jet aircraft. Neither the MS-1 of 1924 nor the Regulus of 1954 were ever used in combat.

RIGHT: THE FIRST MS-1 AT THE NAVY SESQUICENTENNIAL EXPOSITION IN PHILADELPHIA; THE 9-FOOT PROP FROM ANOTHER PLANE PROVIDES SIZE COMPARISON. BELOW: THE FIFTH MS-1 (OF SIX BUILT) SITS ON THE AFTERDECK OF AN S-1 SUBMARINE, BEHIND ITS CYLINDRICAL CONTAINER. OPPOSITE: TWO OF THE SIX MS-1 SUBMARINE OBSERVATION PLANES READY FOR DELIVERY AT THE MARTIN CLEVELAND, OHIO PLANT.

THE CONSOLIDATED XPY-I ADMIRAL

The 1920s saw the advent of a number of large twin-engine flying boats that would be the precursors of the great flying boats of World War II. In the United States, this evolution can be traced to a 1928 US Navy request for proposals for a multi-engine flying boat that would be capable of flying non-stop for 2,000 miles, or the approximate distance between California and Hawaii.

One of the most important flying boats was the Consolidated XPY-1 — not so much for winning the 1928 contract as for its influence on Consolidated designs over the coming decade. Consolidated was formed in 1923 by Reuben Hollis Fleet, a retired US Army Air Corps major. Having passed up offers from both Boeing and Curtiss, he went to work for financially troubled Gallaudet, then located in East Greenwich, Rhode Island. In 1923, after a few months as general manager, he recommended to the directors that the company be liquidated. He told the directors that he would form his own company, and he offered to fulfill the Gallaudet contracts, paying the directors 10 percent of his own net worth to rent the former Gallaudet plant. Fleet invested $15,000 of his own money, along with $10,000 from his sister, Lillian Fleet Bishop, and formed Consolidated. In 1928 Fleet hired I.M. "Mac" Laddon as chief engineer and assigned him to the Navy project.

When it was finished just before Christmas in 1928, the resulting airplane, the XPY-1 Admiral, was billed as "the largest flying boat built in the USA."

The XPY-1 was 61 feet 9 inches in length, 17 feet 4 inches high, and had a wing span of 100 feet. Total wing area was 1,110 square feet. It weighed 8,369 pounds empty, and had a gross weight of 16,492 pounds.

This landmark flying boat was powered by two Pratt & Whitney R-1340-38 Wasp radial engines, each rated at 450 horsepower. This gave the XPY-1 a top speed of 118 mph at sea level, and a cruising speed of 110 mph. It had a service ceiling of 15,300 feet, and its range was 2,620 miles.

Since Lake Erie was frozen, the Admiral was crated and trucked from the Consolidated factory in Buffalo to the Navy test center located in Anacostia, Virginia, where it would be flown in competition with the Martin P3M. For

the first flight on January 10, 1929, the pilot of the Admiral was Navy lieutenant A. W. Gorton. Mac Laddon himself was also aboard. Despite the flight test success of the XPY-1, Martin underbid Consolidated by a half million dollars and won the contract. However, a commercial version of the Admiral, known as the Commodore, was already taking shape.

A footnote to this period of flying boat development involves the Hall-Aluminum Company, founded by Charles Martin Hall, son of the inventor of the aluminum-making process. Acquired by Consolidated in 1940, Hall produced only 29 aircraft, but his methods of aluminum fabrication helped revolutionize the aircraft industry.

RIGHT: THE HALL **XPH-1** WAS FIRST FLOWN IN DECEMBER 1929 AND LED TO A PRODUCTION SERIES OF 29 AIRCRAFT. HALL BECAME PART OF CONSOLIDATED IN 1940. *BELOW:* THE CONSOLIDATED **XPY-1** IS PREPARED FOR A TEST FLIGHT IN FEBRUARY 1929.

THE CONSOLIDATED COMMODORE

In 1928 I.M. "Mac" Laddon and his Consolidated engineering team had responded to a US Navy request for proposals for a multi-engine seaplane capable of flying non-stop for 2,000 miles with the XPY-1 Admiral. Although Consolidated lost the bidding, company president Major Reuben Fleet was encouraged by the success he was having in the commercial airplane market and decided to launch a civilian version of the Admiral.

Known as the Commodore, this aircraft was originally ordered by The Detroit & Cleveland Navigation Company to provide service on Lake Erie. Measuring 61 feet 8 inches in length, 15 feet 8 inches high, the Commodore had a wing span of 100 feet. Total wing area was 1,110 square feet. It weighed 10,550 pounds empty, and had a gross

weight of 17,600 pounds. It could accommodate roughly 22 people depending on interior configuration.

The Commodore was powered by two Pratt & Whiney Hornet B nine-cylinder engines, each rated at 575 horsepower. This gave the aircraft a top speed of 128 mph and a cruising speed of 108 mph. It had a service ceiling of 11,250 feet, and its range was 1,000 miles with space for 650 gallons of fuel.

As the Commodore continued to take shape, Fleet went a step further and teamed up with James H. Rand of Remington Rand to start an airline. In the 1920s, the Atlantic and Pacific were still daunting natural barriers to airline expansion, while Latin America was seen as a land of opportunity. Rand and Fleet sent Captain Ralph O'Neill, a former Army pilot who had been an advisor to the Mexican air corps, on an exploratory mission to South America. Pan American Airways had already established itself as the major airline in the region, but O'Neill managed to line up airmail contracts with the Argentine and Brazilian governments.

In April 1929, Fleet, Rand and O'Neill formed an airline called New York, Rio & Buenos Aires (NYRBA), with service to those three cities as well as others in 15 countries, many of them in the Caribbean. By July 1930, there were seven Commodores on the NYRBA route, which, at 9,000 miles, was the longest in the world. This route had even been the subject of an article in *National Geographic Magazine*.

With the onset of the Great Depression, however, there was financial pressure on NYRBA, and it was sold to Pan American in August 1930. Until 1937, Pan American operated all 14 Commodores. After that date, they were sold to smaller airlines in South America and the Caribbean.

RIGHT: THE PRODUCTION COMMODORES FEA-
TURED A HINGED GLASS AND PLYWOOD CANOPY
FOR THE AIRCREW. *BELOW:* ONE OF TWO EIGHT-
PASSENGER COMPARTMENTS IN THE COMMODORE.
OTHER ACCOMMODATIONS INCLUDED TWO DRAW-
ING ROOMS. *OPPOSITE BOTTOM:* THE **NYRBA**
COMMODORE *HAVANA* OVER LIBERTY ISLAND.

THE MARTIN P3M AND XP2M

The finalists in the first major post-World War I flying boat design competition in the United States were Martin and Consolidated. This 1928 contest for a US Navy contract would initiate a competition that would continue for the remaining history of flying boat production in the United States.

The winning design, the Martin P3M series, was first ordered in June 1929, but the first flight test did not take place until January 26, 1931. Unlike the competing Consolidated XPY-1, the P3M-1 sported an enclosed cockpit. Designed to the same narrow specifications as the Consolidated boat, it was 61 feet 9 inches in length, 16 feet 8 inches high, and had a wing span of 100 feet. Total wing area was 1,115 square feet. It weighed 9,988 pounds empty, and had a gross weight of 15,797 pounds.

The P3M-1 was powered by a pair of Pratt & Whitney R-1340 engines, each rated at 450 horsepower. The production series, however, were designated as P3M-2, and they were powered by a pair of Pratt & Whitney R-1690-32 engines, each rated at 525 horsepower. This gave the aircraft a top speed of 115 mph at sea level. The P3M-1 had a service ceiling of 11,900 feet, and its range was 1,570 miles.

Meanwhile, Martin had gotten a contract to develop a variation on the P3M that would be powered by three Wright R-1820-64 Cyclone engines. On this version, designated XP2M-1, the third cyclone would be positioned above the wing and between the other two. It did offer improved performance, but only one was built. The XP2M-1 had a top speed of 143 mph at sea level, a service ceiling of 13,400 feet, and a maximum range of 1,855 miles.

RIGHT: THE **XP2M-1** (MARTIN MODEL 119), ITS PROPS BARELY TURNING, HAS JUST ALIGHT-ED DURING ROUGH WATER TESTS; NOTE THE FULLY ENCLOSED COCKPIT. *BELOW:* THE ONLY **XP2M-1** BUILT, ON A CHAIN FOR WEIGHING, NEARS COMPLETION. THE THIRD ENGINE WAS LATER REMOVED AND THE AIRCRAFT REDESIG-NATED **XP2M-2**. *OPPOSITE BOTTOM:* THE **P3M-1** TAXIES ON THE WATER DURING ITS SERVICE TESTS IN 1931.

THE MACCHI FLYING BOATS

Toward the end of World War I, when the military seaplanes being developed by the United States, Britain and France were being designed primarily for maritime patrol missions, Italian designers were a good deal more daring. They were also developing innovative, fast seaplanes for aerial combat.

Societa Anonima Macchi was formed in 1912 for the purpose of building the aircraft of the French firm Nieuport who were under license in Italy. These included the well-known Nieuport 11 and Nieuport 17 fighter aircraft, which saw considerable service with Allied air forces during World War I.

In the meantime, Macchi also produced an improved version of the Austrian Lohner flying boat, and this aircraft led to Macchi producing flying boats of its own design.

With its experience building Nieuports, Macchi turned to the idea of flying boat fighters. The Macchi flying boat fighter line was notable for the M.5 single-seater, whose performance matched the better landplane fighters of 1918. Over 270 M.5s were produced by the end of the war.

Adapted from the M.5, the Macchi M.7 was 22 feet 3 inches in length, 9 feet 9 inches high, and had a wing span of 25 feet 5 inches. It weighed 2,270 pounds fully loaded and carried a crew of one. The M.7 was powered by an Isotta-Fraschini Semi-Asso six-cylinder liquid-cooled inline engine, rated at 260 horsepower. This gave the M.7 a top speed of 160 mph, and a service ceiling roughly the same as the M.5's 16,000 feet.

The early Macchi fighters were certainly important for their contributions to the war effort and as a footnote in

aviation history, but also for preparing Macchi for a racing career. In 1921, an M.7 won the important Schneider hydroplane race, an international competition which Macchi seaplanes would come to play an important part for much of the ensuing decade.

The Macchi M.9 reconnaissance flying boat was similar to, but larger than, the M.5 and M.7. It carried a crew of two and was armed with one swiveling, forward-firing machine gun. It measured 31 feet 2 inches in length, 10 feet 4 inches high, and had a wing span of 50 feet 6 inches. It weighed 3,968 pounds.

The M.9 was powered by a Fiat six-cylinder liquid-cooled inline engine, rated at 280 horsepower. This gave the M.9 a top speed of 116 mph, and a service ceiling of 18,050 feet. It had a patrol endurance of four hours.

ABOVE: **THE REMARKABLE MACCHI M.7 SINGLE-SEAT, FLYING BOAT FIGHTER. LIKE ITS SISTER THE M.5, THE M.7 LOOKED SLEEK FOR A FLYING BOAT, BUT WAS CLUMSY FOR A FIGHTER. NEVERTHELESS, IT WAS COMPARED FAVORABLY TO CONTEMPORARY LANDPLANE FIGHTERS. THE M.7 WON THE 1921 SCHNEIDER CUP.**

THE VOUGHT O2U CORSAIR

Often called the most important US Navy observation seaplane of the pre-World War II era, the Vought O2U Corsair evolved from the Vought VE-7, which was the first American floatplane launched routinely from the compressed-air catapults of major capital ships such as battleships and cruisers.

Based on a US Army landplane trainer, the VE-7 floatplane joined the Navy Fleet in 1920, and th Corsair made its first catapult-launch from the deck of the then-new battleship USS *Maryland* on May 24, 1922. Ultimately the Navy would acquire 60 VE-7s from Vought and build 69 at the Naval Aircraft Factory.

The successor to the VE-7 was the UO-1, of which Vought built 140 between 1922 and 1927. In 1926, Vought president Chance Vought proposed a new observation floatplane to the Navy that would be designed around the new Pratt & Whitney Wasp radial engine. The Navy accepted the proposal and ordered it under the designation O2U-1. The first prototype flew on November 2, 1926, and 130 were purchased to equip every cruiser and battleship in the fleet.

Some O2U-1 Corsairs were delivered as landplanes for use by the US Marine Corps, as were most of the 37 O2U-2s. These were deployed to Nicaragua and Haiti, where the Marines had been sent to help chase bandits. One Marine earned the Congressional Medal of Honor for a rescue mission flown in a Corsair.

The production run also included 80 O2U-3s and 42 O2U-4s, all of which were delivered by the end of 1930.

Export customers for the Corsair included Argentina, Brazil, Canada, Cuba and Peru, as well as Mexico, where they were also built under license. In Japan, the Nakajima company copied the Corsair as the basis for their Type 90-II.

Chiang Kai-shek's Chinese Nationalist government bought 20, one of which scored the Corsair's first aerial victory in combat with a Junkers W.33 belonging to a rival warlord. Corsairs also participated in the defense of Shanghai against the Japanese in 1937.

In seaplane configuration, the O2U-3 and O2U-4 were slightly larger than the O2U-1, measuring 28 feet 10 inches in length, 11 feet 6 inches high, and with a wing span of 36 feet. Total wing area was 318.5 square feet. It weighed 2,518 pounds empty, and had a gross weight of 3,995 pounds. All Corsairs were powered by the Pratt & Whitney R-1340C Wasp engine, rated at 450 horsepower.

Top speed ratings clocked from 136 mph for the O2U-3 to 149 mph for the O2U-1. The range of the O2U-4 was 495 miles compared to 632 for the O2U-3. The service ceilings ranged from 16,100 feet for the O2U-3 to 18,700 feet for the O2U-1. Armament consisted of a forward-firing Browning machine gun on the top wing.

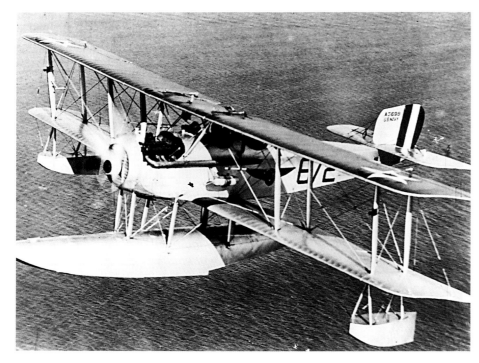

RIGHT: AN O2U-4 TOUCHING DOWN ON THE WATER. *BELOW:* AN O2U-1 FROM THE HEAVY CRUISER USS *RALEIGH.* AT ONE TIME CORSAIRS SERVED ABOARD EVERY CRUISER AND BATTLESHIP IN THE US FLEET. NOTE THE DIFFERENCE IN THE TAIL BETWEEN THE O2U-1 AND O2U-4. *OPPOSITE BOTTOM:* THE VE-7 WAS THE US NAVY'S FIRST WIDELY-USED FLOATPLANE.

SEAPLANES FOR THE SCHNEIDER RACE

The years after World War I were marked by a great celebration of flight, and one of the important aspects of this fixation were the international meets and air races. One of the most interesting series of recurring air races were Schneider Trophy seaplane races, a brainchild of French arms-maker and aviation patron Jacques Schneider.

The Schneider Trophy Races of the 1920s and 1930s are remembered as some of the greatest moments in seaplane history. However, the race actually dated back to before World War I, with the first two having been held in 1913 and 1914 at Monaco. The races resumed in 1919 amid a row between Britain and Italy over who would host the race. Britain won that contest, but the race turned into a farce when the only plane to finish, an Italian Savoia S.13, was compelled to make an extra lap in order to win the trophy. It ran out of fuel in the process, and there were no official finishers.

The Macchi M.7 was the winner in 1921, when the race was held in the Adriatic off Venice. The next year, Briton Henri Baird took the trophy to England with a 146 mph win at Naples. Baird's aircraft was a Supermarine Sea Lion II, a remarkable plane that was to be a precursor to the Supermarine seaplanes that would dominate the final years of the Schneider Trophy Race in the 1930s.

By the following year, a growing interest in air races and demonstration flying in the United States led the US Navy to enter the Schneider Trophy Race with a pair of Curtiss CR-3s, specifically designed as race planes.

In retrospect, it may seem strange or even extravagant that the US Navy should invest in building an aircraft specifically for air racing. It was similar to the US Army's odd fixation with fielding teams in competitive polo. However, it was seen as a good exercise in developing fast and maneuverable high-performance aircraft. Then too, there was the prestige aspect of the competition. The Pulitzer races that were held during this era turned into a duel between the Army and the Navy, who were constantly trying to outdo one another.

The US Navy became so involved in racing that, from 1922 to 1928, they actually assigned an official "racer" designation in their nomenclature. When Congress looked askance at this practice a few years later, race planes started receiving "fighter" designations.

The three aircraft types to receive the "racer" designation were all from Curtiss: the CR, the R2C and the R3C. The latter two later became F2C and F3C, respectively. The first CR, the CR-1, was built specifically for the 1921 Pulitzer Race. Powered by a 405 horsepower Curtiss CD12 engine, it came in first. In 1922, the Navy raced another CR-1, plus a CR-2, which was actually a modified CR-1. After they came in a disappointing third and fourth in the race, the Navy changed engines and developed the CR-3. It was 25 feet 10 inches in length, 10 feet high, from the top of its tail to the bottom of its pontoons, and had a wing span of 22 feet 8 inches. It had a gross weight of 2,746 pounds, and was powered by a 450 horsepower Curtiss D-12 liquid-cooled V-12 engine that gave it a top speed of 188 mph. The CR-3 had a range of 520 miles.

Two CR-3s were entered in September 1923's Schneider Trophy Race, held near Cowes on Britain's Isle of Wight. Navy Lieutenant David Rittenhouse took the Trophy in a CR-3, at a speed of 181.029 mph. He edged out Lieutenant Rutledge Irvine in the other CR-3. This

RIGHT: **THE CURTISS R3C-2 THAT WON THE 1925 SCHNEIDER TROPHY.** *BELOW:* **THE 1926 WINNING TEAM AND THEIR MACCHI M.39.**

stunning performance buoyed the spirits of those at the Navy's Bureau of Aeronautics. A month later, a pair of R2Cs took the top spots at the Pulitzer Race in St. Louis. On October 6, 1923, Lieutenant Alford Williams set a new world speed record of 243.63 mph in his R2C, followed by Lieutenant Harold Brow in another R2C — who also beat the previous world record — with a speed of 241.74 mph.

The 1924 Schneider Trophy Race was called off because the British and Italian aircraft were "not ready," and the Americans agreed to a postponement. This set the stage for an interesting race which would pit Italy's Macchi M.33, Britain's Gloster IIA and new Supermarine S.4 monoplane against the latest of the racers that Curtiss was developing for the US Navy.

The Curtiss R3C-2 designed for the 1925 Schneider Trophy event was a trim biplane with a wing span of 22 feet, and a length of 22 feet. It weighed 2,738 pounds fully loaded and fueled, and was powered by a 565 horsepower Curtiss V-1400 liquid-cooled V-12 engine that gave it a top speed of 245 mph. The R3C-2 had a range of 290 miles. At the controls for the race would be an Army, rather than Navy, pilot. Army test pilot Lieutenant Jimmy Doolittle was at the threshold of an aviation career that would flourish 15 years later during World War II.

The 1925 Schneider was held on Chesapeake Bay. It was the first of only two Schneider Trophy Races hosted by the United States. The Supermarine entry, whose cantilever wing was apt to flutter, stalled out and side-slipped into the water. The Macchi came in third, and the Gloster was second. Doolittle piloted the R3C to victory with a speed of 232.57 mph. He was the only pilot to break the 200 mph mark. Ironically, it had been an Army pilot who navigated a Navy Curtiss racer to its final international triumph.

The 1926 Schneider Race was held off Hampton Roads, Virginia, near the Norfolk Navy Yard. The Italian government had taken a keen interest in the race and had appropriated a great deal of research and development money for the new Macchi M.39 monoplane, as well as the powerful 800 horsepower, 12-cylinder Fiat AS.2 inline engine.

The Macchi M.39 was 22 feet 1 inch in length, 9 feet 9 inches high, and had a wing span of 30 feet 4.5 inches. It weighed 2,772 pounds empty, and had a gross weight of 3,465 pounds. The Fiat AS.2 gave it a top speed rating of

272 mph. The home team, the US Navy, fielded an R3C-2 and an R3C-4, which was an R3C-3 with a 700 horsepower Curtiss V-1550 engine.

Held on November 13, 1926, it was the fastest Schneider Trophy Race to date. In the R3C-2, US Navy Lieutenant George Cuddihy managed to reach a speed of 232.42 mph, but ran out of fuel before he crossed the finish line. The Italian investment paid off, as Major Mario di Bernardi's bright red Macchi M.39 won the race with a speed of 246.5 mph. A second M.39, piloted by Adriano Bacula, came in third with a speed of 218 mph. This would be the last Schneider Trophy Race for the Curtiss racers and for the United States. The official explanation was that costs were prohibitive.

For the 1927 Schneider Race, Reginald J. Mitchell, the top designer for Supermarine, threw away all the preconceptions and created an amazing new aircraft. As with the Macchi a year earlier, Supermarine applied the best leading edge technology and created what would prove to be the best racing seaplane in the world. The Royal Air Force, meanwhile, set up a special High-Speed Flight to train crews and prepare aircraft.

The Supermarine S.5 was 24 feet 3.5 inches in length, 11 feet 1 inch high, and had a wing span of 26 feet 9 inches. It weighed 2,680 pounds empty, and had a gross weight of 3,242 pounds. The S.5 was powered by a Napier Lion VIIB 12-cylinder broad arrow, liquid-cooled engine, rated at 875 horsepower. This gave it a recorded top speed of 319.57 mph.

The 1927 race returned to Venice with the Italians as

RIGHT AND BELOW: REGINALD MITCHELL'S WONDERFUL-
LY SLEEK SUPERMARINE S.5 WAS THE STAR OF THE SHOW
WHEN BRITAIN WON THE 1927 SCHNEIDER TROPHY
RACE.

defending champions. They fielded three Macchi M.52s, an improved version of the great M.39. The British entered three of the new Supermarine S.5s, as well as an equal number of Gloster IV biplanes.

Taking place on September 26, the race was dominated by the S.5s. S.N. Webster won the race with a speed of 281.655 mph, and O.E. Worsley posted a speed of 273.07 mph to take second place.

The next Schneider Trophy Race was held in 1929, the decision having been made to hold the event biannually. Again Reginald Mitchell pulled out all the stops to create the best floatplane racer possible, the Supermarine S.6, powered by a supercharged 1,900-horsepower Rolls Royce engine.

This time, Britain was the defending champion, and the race occurred on September 7 off the coast of Southampton in southern England. Royal Air Force Flying Officer H.R.D. Waghorn won the race, achieving a speed of 328.629 mph in his S.6. His victory was marred only by his suffering the embarrassment of his engine dying as he took his victory lap. Waghorn had lost count of the laps and thought that this was the final lap of the race. He was quite relieved to find out that he had actually won the race before the mishap.

The Italian team was not so lucky. Severe engine trouble dogged their Macchi M.67s, filling the cockpits with exhaust fumes and blinding the pilots. One of the Italian pilots was also severely burned by engine coolant.

The 1931 Schneider Trophy Race, held September 13 near Calshot off the coast of Hampshire, was once again a showcase for one of Mitchell's amazing Supermarine racers, an improved variant of the S.6. The Supermarine S.6B was 28 feet 10 inches in length, 12 feet 3 inches high, and had a wing span of 26 feet 9 inches. Weighing 4,590 pounds empty, it had a gross weight of 6,086 pounds.

The S.6B was powered by a Rolls Royce 12-cylinder V, liquid-cooled engine, rated at 2,350 horsepower, and giving the aircraft a top speed in excess of 400 mph. At this speed, however, the engine could be expected to overheat and self-destruct after an hour of full throttle. It was built for speed, not durability.

As it turned out, however, the French and Italian teams did not have their aircraft ready in time, and the S.6B flew only against the clock. Captain John Boothman achieved a speed of 340.08 mph as Britain became the only nation to win the Schneider three times in a row. This permanently retired the Schneider Trophy, and ended the greatest series of seaplane races in history.

The Supermarine S.6B went on to set a top speed of 407.05 mph, and to form the basis for Reginald Mitchell's greatest achievement, the legendary Supermarine Spitfire fighter that would become a World War II legend as the aircraft that won the Battle of Britain and saved England.

Right and Below: **The Supermarine S.6 won the 1929 Schneider Trophy Race with a speed of 328.629 mph, but pilot H.R.D. Waghorn suffered an engine failure during his victory lap.**

THE DORNIER DO.X

Claudius Dornier began his aviation career in 1910 as a designer with Zeppelin-Werke GmbH, working on airships and flying boats. After World War I, he formed his own company to produce the highly successful Dornier Wal (Whale), discussed in detail on the following spread.

In 1926, Dornier started work on what was the largest aircraft that had ever been produced to that date. The gargantuan Do.X was, given its size in relation to anything that had yet to be imagined, the most ambitious — in terms of matching existing technology to ambition — flying boat project ever to be built, with the possible exception of Howard Hughes' massive "Spruce Goose" project.

Dornier was not the only aircraft designer in the 1920s to dream of crossing the Atlantic in a colossal ocean liner of the air — American designer Norman Bel Geddes designed a 450-passenger monster — but he was the only one to actually see his dream fulfilled.

Finally completed in 1929, the Do.X was 131 feet 4.75 inches in length, 29 feet 6 inches high, and had a wing span of 157 feet 5.75 inches. It had a gross weight of 114,640 pounds and could accommodate up to 100 passengers — in luxurious lounges and staterooms — and a crew of 10. The Do.X made its first flight on July 25, lifting off Lake Constance on the Swiss-German border.

RIGHT: THE INTERNAL CONFIGURATION OF THE
DORNIER DO.X WAS MODELED AFTER THAT OF AN
OCEAN LINER. THE SIMILARITY WAS NOT COINCI-
DENTAL, AS CLAUDIUS DORNIER HOPED TO MAR-
KET HIS BIG SHIP TO THE WELL-HEELED TRAVELER
INTERESTED IN BOTH LUXURY AND SPEED.
BELOW: THE DO.X STARTS OUT ON ITS GRAND
PUBLICITY TOUR OF 1930-1932. IT MATCHED THE
EXPANSIVE MOOD OF THE ROARING TWENTIES, BUT
UNFORTUNATELY IT HAD LITTLE PLACE IN THE GRIM
DEPTHS OF THE GREAT DEPRESSION.

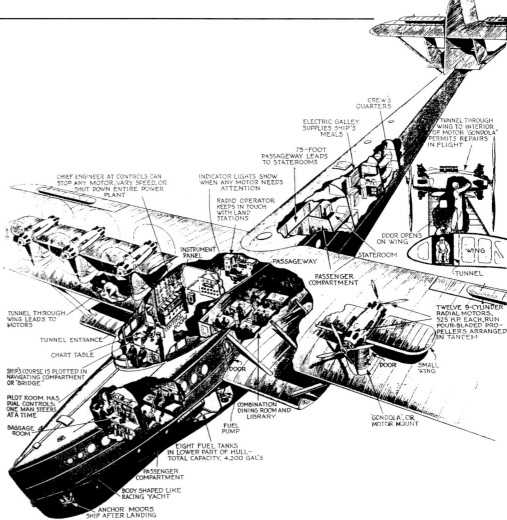

It was initially powered by 12 Bristol Jupiter liquid-cooled engines, arranged in pairs and each rated at 575 horsepower. This was the largest number of engines that would ever be used to power a production airplane. Even the great Consolidated B-36 of the 1950s had only 10. The Jupiters would later be replaced by 12 American-made Curtiss Conqueror V-12 liquid-cooled engines, each rated at 600 horsepower. This complement would give the big airplane a cruising speed of 118 mph. It had a range of 1,056 miles.

The Do.X carried passengers for the first time in October 1929, and undertook a round-the-world publicity tour in November 1930. It suffered fire and hull damage in Portugal, but finally arrived in New York in August 1931.

The big flying boat finally returned to Friedrichshafen in May 1932, after 19 months and just two commercial orders. The Italian airline SA Navigazione Aerea (SANA) ordered a pair for use on its Trieste-Venice-Genoa-Marseilles-Barcelona-Gibraltar-Cadiz route.

They were intended to be named after the great Italian pilots Alessandro Guidoni and Umberto Maddalena, and they would have become commercial aviation legends. However, the two Do.Xs were diverted from airline use by the Italian air force, used briefly, and then unceremoniously destroyed.

THE DORNIER WAL

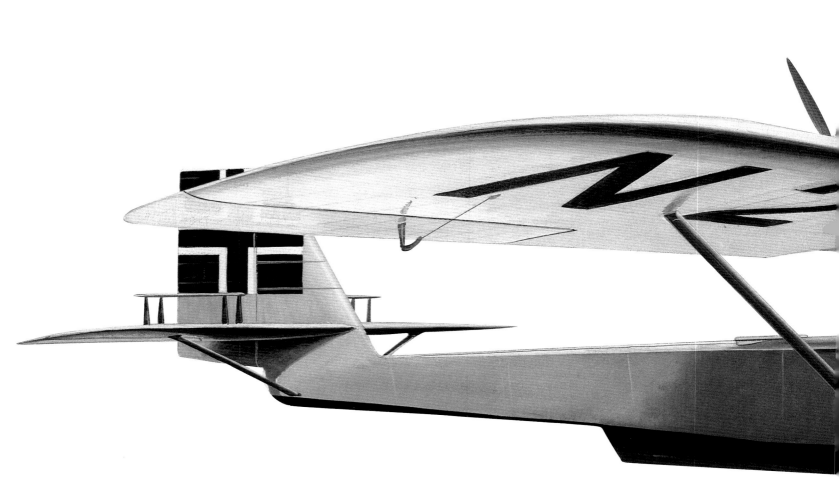

The most successful project undertaken by Dornier-Werke before World War II, the Do.J Wal (Whale) was the brainchild of company founder Claudius Dornier.

Having learned the trade at Zeppelin-Werke before and during World War I, Dornier launched his own firm in 1920 with the Do.L Delphin (Dolphin) flying boat. Sold mainly to German domestic air services, the Delphin was an all-metal monoplane with an entirely enclosed cabin, unlike the later Wal, whose flight deck was open to the elements in the manner preferred by pilots of the era, who liked the feel of the slipstream on their faces.

The Do.L Delphin was powered by a BMW IV six-cylinder liquid cooled engine rated at 300 horsepower. It had a cruising speed of 78 mph and a service ceiling of 9,800 feet.

The Dornier Delphin remained in production through 1928, but its modest sales never matched the success enjoyed by the Do.J Wal. First flown on November 1922, the Do.J Wal was created against the backdrop of severe limitations placed on German aviation imposed by the victorious Allies under the Treaty of Versailles. German air power had been such a potent force during the war that the Allies wanted to keep the once robust industry down through limitations on aircraft manufacturing.

By 1922, under the Treaty of Versailles, the Wal prototype, which had been built in Germany, had to be shipped to Italy to be launched. Eventually, about half of the 300 Wals that were produced were manufactured in Italy by Construzzioni Meccaniche Aeronautiche in Pisa. Wals were also to be produced under license in Spain and

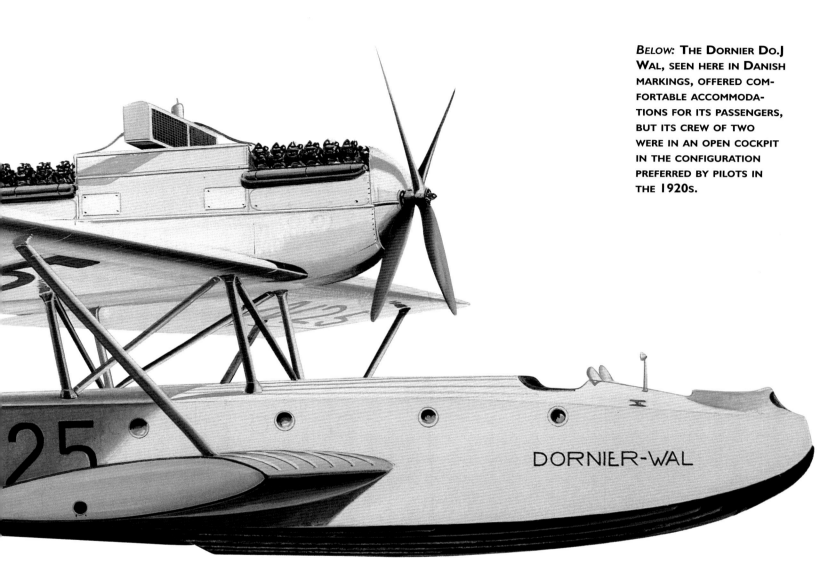

the Netherlands, and they would find customers throughout Europe and as far away as Brazil and Japan.

Constructed of light Duralumin, the Wal was 56 feet 7.25 inches in length, 17 feet high, and had a wing span of 73 feet 10 inches. It weighed 12,566 pounds and accommodated up to 10 passengers. The Wal was powered by two engines, one pushing, one pulling in a single nacelle. Various engines used included those manufactured by Hispano-Suiza and Lorraine in France, Fiat in Italy and Britain's Rolls Royce. A popular powerplant system was a pair of Rolls Royce Eagle IX 12-cylinder liquid-cooled engines, each rated at 360 horsepower. This gave it a cruising speed of 87 mph. The Wal had a service ceiling of 11,480 feet, and its range was 1,350 miles. Dornier would continue to

produce the Wal until 1936, having introduced the Do.R Super Wal in 1926. This flying boat was powered by four 500-horsepower Bristol Jupiter VIII radial engines.

Between May and July 1925, Arctic explorers Roald Amundsen and Lincoln Elsworth used a pair of ice-adapted Dornier Wals in their expedition to the North Pole. Caught in fog, they were forced down, but managed to rescue their team using one of the Wals.

By 1927, the German airline Deutsche Luft Hansa (now Lufthansa) was using the Wal on its service to Norway and Sweden, as well as on its South Atlantic route to Natal in Brazil. Ultimately, Wals would make 328 Atlantic crossings, an outstanding accomplishment for the late 1920s and early 1930s.

THE DOUGLAS XO2D

Founded by Donald Douglas in 1920 at Los Angeles, California, the Douglas Aircraft Company grew from modest beginnings to become one of the most important builders of both military and commercial aircraft in the world.

The first Douglas airplane, the Cloudster, was built to be the first to cross North America non-stop. This was not accomplished, but Douglas used the experience to enter — and win — a Navy competition for a seaplane torpedo bomber. Under the designations DT-1 and DT-2, the Navy ordered 42 of these pontoon-equipped seaplanes.

In 1929, Douglas moved his factory to Clover Field in Santa Monica, California, then a small town between downtown Los Angeles and the Pacific coast. Here the company produced a wide variety of single-engine biplanes, including the PD-1 open-cockpit amphibian and the T2D, a twin-engine, twin-pontoon torpedo bomber. One of the most ambitious Douglas projects was the Douglas World Cruiser,

built for the US Army and used for an epic 1924 flight around the world. Based on the Navy DT-2, the cruisers were designed to be converted back and forth from land-planes to seaplanes as they made their flight.

The final Douglas floatplane was the XO2D, created for US Navy evaluation in 1934. It is pictured here as an example of state of the art American floatplane design at the end of the biplane era. It was 32 feet in length, 16 feet 4 inches high, and had a wing span of 36 feet with the folding wings fully extended. Total wing area was 302.8 square feet. Weighing 3,460 pounds empty, it had a gross weight of 5,109 pounds. Like its competition, the Curtiss XO3C-1 and the Vought XO5U-1, the XO2D-1 was powered by a Pratt & Whitney R-1340-12 radial engine, rated at 550 horsepower. This gave the XO2D-1 a top speed of 162 mph at sea level, and a cruising speed of 158 mph at 5,000 feet. It had a service ceiling of 14,300 feet, and its range was 798 miles.

ABOVE AND FACING PAGE: VIEWS OF THE XO2D-1 TAKEN AT CLOVER FIELD IN SANTA MONICA, CALIFORNIA IN MARCH 1934.

5906
XO2D-1
3.27.34

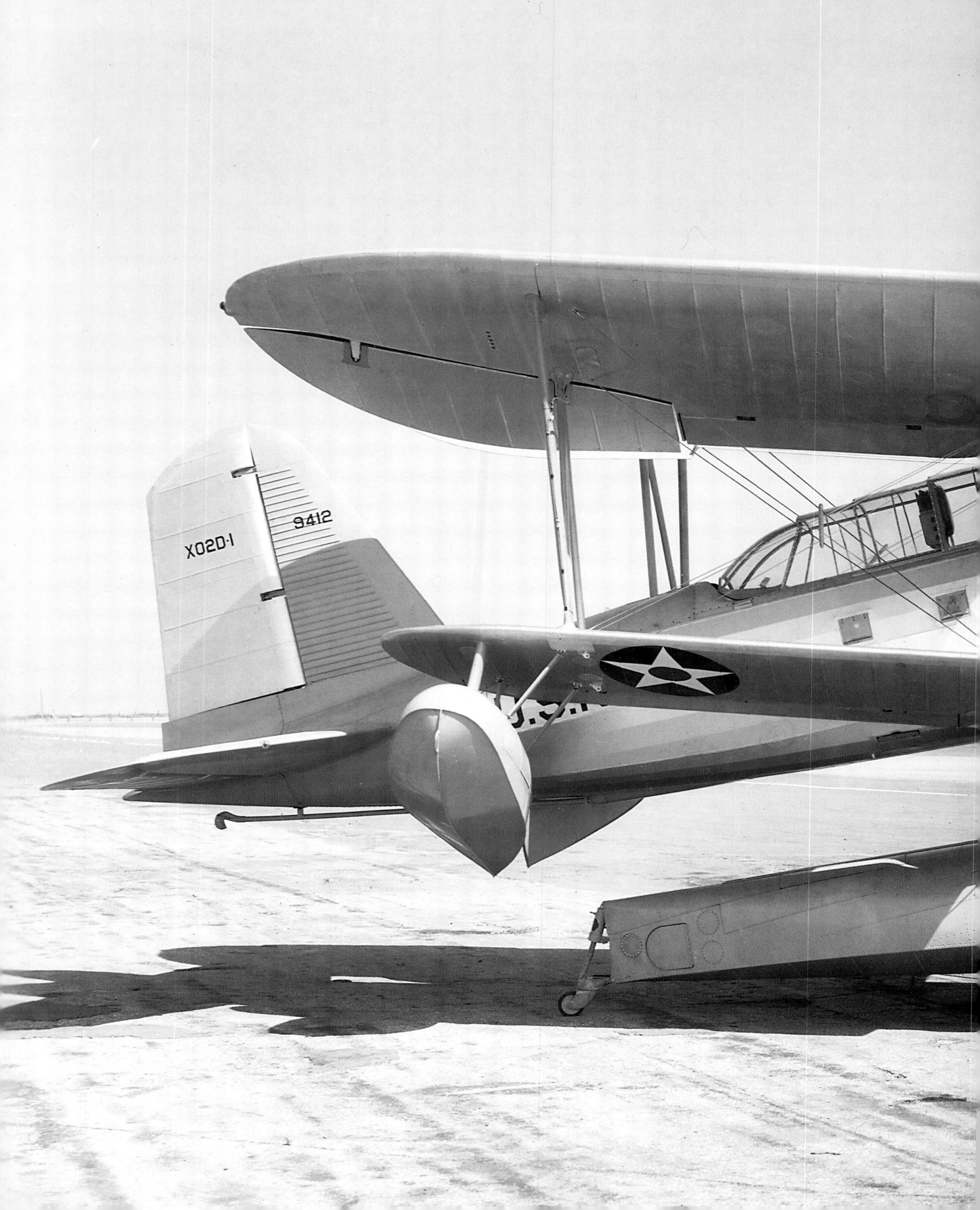
9412
X02D-1

Below: THE XO2D-1 WITH ITS WINGS FOLDED AS THEY WOULD BE FOR STORAGE ABOARD A SHIP. THE LANDING GEAR SYSTEM, IN WHICH THE WHEELS FOLDED NEATLY INTO THE PONTOON, ADDRESSED THE US NAVY REQUIREMENT THAT THE AIRCRAFT BE AMPHIBIOUS. MOST FLOATPLANES OF THE ERA WERE NOT AMPHIBIOUS BECAUSE THE WHEELS AND THE COMPLEX RETRACTION GEAR ADDED BOTH WEIGHT AND COST.

THE LATÉCOÈRE FLYING BOATS

Both the style and ambition of French flying boat design in the years between the two world wars reached their apogee in the grand and beautiful machines that bore the name Latécoère.

As aircraft evolved in the 1920s and 1930s, the Europeans developed an interest in Transatlantic air travel. The aircraft that helped make this a reality included the German Dorniers and those produced by Latécoère in France.

The Latécoère 300 was created in response to a French government request for an aircraft that could carry a ton of mail across the South Atlantic. The prototype, known as *Croix du Sud* (*Southern Cross*), entered service in December 1933 with a record-setting 24-hour, 2,285-mile flight from Marseilles to Senegal. The *Croix du Sud* went on to serve the route between Dakar and Natal, Brazil until December 1936, when it was lost at sea.

In the meantime, Latécoère delivered three production aircraft to Air France and three to the French Navy.

The Latécoère 300 was 85 feet 11.5 inches in length, 20 feet 11 inches high, and had a wing span of 145 feet. It had a gross weight of 50,706 pounds. The Latécoère 300 was powered by four Hispano-Suiza 12N 12-cylinder liquid-cooled engines, each rated at 650 horsepower. This gave it a cruising speed of 99.4 mph. It had a service ceiling of 15,090 feet, and its range was 2,982 miles with 2,204 pounds of cargo.

In 1936, the much larger Latécoère 521 was unveiled. Designed for the longer North Atlantic route, it was nearly as large as the great Dornier Do.X of 1929. Damaged by a typhoon on its first transocean flight, the prototype had to be rebuilt and did not complete a flight to New York until August 1938. Although Air France bought one Latécoère 521, World War II began before it entered service. The Latécoère 521 was 103 feet 9 inches in length, 29 feet 9 inches high, and had a wing span of 161 feet 9.25 inches. It had a gross weight of 83,627 pounds. The Latécoère 521 was powered by six Hispano-Suiza 12Y 12-cylinder engines, each rated at 860 horsepower, giving it a cruising speed of 130 mph. It had a service ceiling of 20,669, feet, and it carried 30 to 70 passengers up to 2,547 miles.

BELOW: **THE RECORD-SETTING LATÉCOÈRE 300 FLYING BOAT** *CROIX DU SUD* **IN THE WATER AT NATAL IN BRAZIL. IT WAS LOST AT SEA WITH ALL HANDS ON DECEMBER 7, 1936.**

THE CONSOLIDATED P2Y RANGER

Just as the experience of the XPY-1 led the Consolidated Aircraft Corporation to build the Commodore commercial transport, so too did the apparent success of the Commodore give Consolidated another chance at a Navy flying boat contract.

The next US Navy design competition after the one in which the Martin P3M beat the Consolidated XPY-1 was scheduled for 1931. Reuben Fleet and Mac Laddon redesigned the Commodore, creating a *sesquiplane* version, a flying boat with abbreviated lower wings, each mounted with pontoons. In May 1931, the Navy ordered a prototype XP2Y, and in July they placed an order that would lead to 47 of the new planes being delivered under the designation P2Y, also known as the Ranger.

The first production P2Y Rangers started flying for the Navy in 1933, and in September of that year, Lieutenant Commander Knefler McGinnis led a squadron of six P2Ys 2,059 miles from Norfolk to the Coco Solo Naval Air Station in the Panama Canal Zone non-stop. In January 1934, McGinnis and his squadron flew 2,408 miles from San Francisco to Hawaii, the longest over-water, formation flight ever accomplished.

The Ranger was 61 feet 9 inches in length, 17 feet 3 inches high, and had a wing span of 100 feet. Total wing area measured 1,430 square feet. Weighing 10,950 pounds empty, it had a gross weight of 19,852 pounds. The P2Y-1 was powered by a pair of Wright R-1820-E Cyclone engines, each rated at 575 horsepower. This gave the aircraft a top speed of 126 mph at sea level. It had a service ceiling of 11,200 feet, and its range was 2,050 miles.

In 1933, one XP2Y-2 was adapted from the last P2Y-1 by retrofitting R-1820-88 Cyclones. There were no production P2Y-2s, but the Navy did order 23 P2Y-3s, which were powered by a pair of Wright R-1820-90 Cyclones, each rated at 750 horsepower. This gave the aircraft a top speed of 139 mph at sea level. The P2Y-3 had a service ceiling of 16,100 feet, and its range was 1,180 miles with space for 2,000 pounds of bombs.

In addition to US Navy orders, Rangers were sold to Columbia, Argentina and Japan. In the latter country, the Ranger was copied to form the basis of the Kawanishi H6K flying boat, which would see service in World War II.

The Ranger series was the last major aircraft program to be undertaken by Consolidated before the firm moved its center of operations from Buffalo, New York to San Diego, California. When a company is in the flying boat business and its factory is located on a lake that freezes in the winter, it doesn't take long to recognize that it's time to look for a new location. The move to the West Coast would be complete, and a new factory humming, by October 1935.

RIGHT: ONE OF THE US NAVY'S P2Y-3s ON PATROL. BELOW: THE XP2Y-1 PROTOTYPE. THE SNOW AND ICE SEEN HERE LED TO CONSOLIDATED ABANDONING NEW YORK STATE. OPPOSITE BOTTOM: THERE WAS ONLY ONE XP2Y-2 PRODUCED, BUT IT LED TO A US NAVY ORDER FOR 23 P2Y-3s. OVERLEAF: THE ARGENTINE NAVY TOOK DELIVERY OF THREE P2Y-3s BETWEEN JUNE AND AUGUST 1937.

THE SAVOIA MARCHETTI S.55

The Savoia Marchetti S.55 is probably the signature flying boat in Italian aviation history. It is remembered both for an unusual design and for epic overseas flights that often involved massed formations of S.55s.

In 1923, Marchetti designed the aircraft for Societa Idrovolanti Alto Italia (Savoia) in response to an Italian government request for proposals for a flying boat patrol bomber. Marchetti's innovative design eliminated the use of a central fuselage, locating the crew and cargo compartments in the two large pontoons which were, in effect, a pair of 30-foot, fully-enclosed boats. Across the two boats, he mounted a broad, thick wing which contained the flight deck. Like its smaller predecessors, but unlike other large flying boats of the era, the S.55's wings and twin hulls were constructed entirely of wood.

The S.55P prototype first flew in August 1924, and promptly set 14 world speed and distance records for its class. In 1927, Francesco de Pinedo and Carlo del Prete flew a Series 1 S.55 nicknamed *Santa Maria* on a 27,230-mile flight around the Atlantic Ocean. The following year, the aviators Umberto Maddalena and Stefano Cagno used an S.55 in the search for the dirigible that crashed in the Arctic with explorer Umberto Nobile and his expedition aboard.

The most famous exploits of the S.55 were the great mass demonstration flights engineered by General Italo Balbo, commander of the Regia Aeronautica (Italian Air Force). In December 1930, Balbo led a formation of 14 S.55s out of Orbatello, north of Rome, on a 6,462-mile flight to Rio de Janiero. Three of the aircraft were forced to turn back, but the Brazilians had never witnessed such an aerial spectacle of

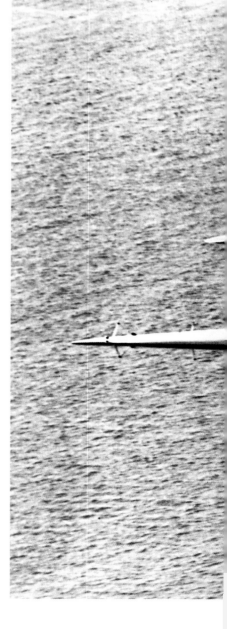

RIGHT: **ONE OF GENERAL ITALO BALBO'S MASSED FOR-MATIONS OF S.55S.** *BELOW:* **AN S.55 IN FLIGHT OVER THE MEDITERRANEAN.** *OPPOSITE BOTTOM:* **AN S.55 OF THE REGIA AERONAUTICA WITH ITS FLAG WAVING IN THE BREEZE.**

the magnitude of Balbo's formation thundering over the city on January 15, 1931.

In 1933, to celebrate the tenth anniversary of the Regia Aeronautica, Balbo took a group of 25 S.55s on a demonstration flight to the Chicago World's Fair. They arrived in the skies over the Windy City on July 15, after stops in Amsterdam, Ireland, Iceland and Montreal. From Chicago, they flew to New York, returning to Europe by way of the Azores, where one plane was lost.

Their triumphant return to Rome after the 12,300-mile trip was greeted by Romans in a celebration that press releases compared to the spectacle of Constantine welcoming the return of the Roman Legions.

Between 1926 and 1937, commercial variants of the S.55 were also in service on air routes in the Mediterranean. Operated by such airlines as Aero Espresso, Ala Littoria and Societa Aerea Mediterranea. The commercial variants accommodated eight to 10 passengers, depending on configuration.

The final version was the S.55X, which was introduced in 1933. this variant had more powerful engines and a longer unrefuelled range.

The aircraft of the S.55 series were 54 feet 1.5 inches in length, 16 feet 5 inches high, and had a wing span of 78 feet 9 inches. The S.55P weighed 16,534 pounds, the S.55 1 *Santa Maria* 14,343 pounds and the S.55X 22,000 pounds. Each aircraft in the series was powered by a pair of Isotta-Fraschini Asso engines. The two earlier models used the 12-cylinder water-cooled type 500, each rated at 500 horsepower, while the S.55X used an 18 cylinder broad arrow liquid-cooled type rated at 750 horsepower.

The S.55P had a cruising speed of 106 mph, a service ceiling of 8,694 feet, and its range was 621 miles. The S.55 1 *Santa Maria* possessed a cruising speed of 103 mph, a service ceiling of 9,845 feet, and an endurance of six hours, while the S.55X had a cruising speed of 149 mph, a service ceiling of 16,400 feet, and its range was 2,400 miles — more than double that of the S.55P of seven years earlier.

The successor to the S.55 was the three-engine S.66, introduced in 1933. The engines were 12-cylinder, liquid-cooled, 750-horsepower Fiat A.24Rs. The S.66 was configured exactly like the S.55, except for the engines and tail surfaces, and it was 54 feet 6.75 inches in length, 16 feet 2 inches high, with a wing span of 108 feet 3.25 inches. It weighed 24,140 pounds, had a cruising speed of 138 mph, a service ceiling of 18,050 feet, and a range of 800 miles.

With a passenger capacity of 14 to 18, the S.66 flew throughout the Mediterranean — from Gibraltar to Haifa — with such Italian air carriers as Aero Espresso, Ala Littoria, Navigazione Aerea and Societa Aerea Mediterranea.

RIGHT: **A HEAD-ON ROSTER VIEW OF AN S.55X WITH ITS 18-CYLINDER ISOTTA FRASCHINI ENGINES.** *BELOW:* **AN S.55 COMING IN FOR A LANDING ON AN ITALIAN LAKE.**

THE SIKORSKY S-38

He designed the biggest bombers in the world for the last Tsar of Imperial Russia and he invented the practical helicopter. In between, Igor Sikorsky produced a family of durable seaplanes that helped Pan American Airways become one of the first major players in routine transocean airline service.

Sikorsky moved his company to the United States after the Russian Revolution, and in the early 1920s he focussed on producing large biplane transports. His first seaplanes were one each of the S-32 and S-34, both built in 1926. The latter was a direct precursor to the S-38, which first flew in 1928.

The same year, Pan American acquired three S-38As, the first of its fleet of 38 S-38s, for use on its routes in Central America. On February 4, Charles Lindbergh flew a Pan Am S-38 on the first airmail flight to Panama, and then toured the Caribbean on a demonstration flight. In 1929, Reuben Fleet's New York, Rio & Buenos Aires (NYRBA) air service also acquired one, which joined Pan American when it absorbed NYRBA in 1930. It was also in 1929 that Inter-Island Airways in Hawaii selected the S-38 to help

inaugurate service between Honolulu and the islands of Maui, Kauai and Hawaii.

Martin and Osa Johnson, producers of popular books and films about wildlife, purchased a pair of S-38s, which they used for many years in their work throughout Africa and Southeast Asia. One of them, called *Osa's Ark,* appeared in the films painted in broad zebra stripes.

The S-38 was to be the most successful fixed wing (non-helicopter) in Sikorsky history, with 111 of them produced for commercial customers, as well as the United States military services under the PS and C-6 designations.

The S-38 was 40 feet 3 inches in length, 13 feet 10 inches high, had an upper wing span of 71 feet 8 inches, and the span of the lower wing was 36 feet. It weighed 6,850 pounds empty and had a gross weight of 10,480 pounds. The S-38 was powered by a pair of Pratt & Whitney Wasp radial engines, each rated at 575 horsepower. These enabled a cruising speed of 103 mph. Early S-38s had a service ceiling of 16,000 feet, while the S-38C had a service ceiling of 18,000 feet. All aircraft possessed a range of up to 600 miles.

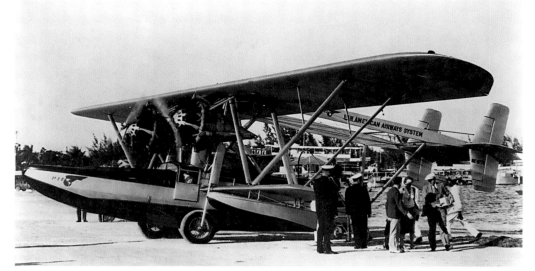

RIGHT: ONE OF PAN AMERICAN'S S-38S PREPARES FOR A FLIGHT. *BELOW:* THE COMFORTABLE INTERIOR ARRANGEMENT OF A PRIVATELY-OWNED S-38. *OPPOSITE BOTTOM:* THE SIKORSKY S-38 WAS A SESQUIPLANE RATHER THAN A BIPLANE BECAUSE ITS LOWER WING WAS MUCH SHORTER THAN THE UPPER.

THE SHORT EMPIRE FLYING BOATS

While there was a strong interest in long range airliners among the French, Germans, Italians and Americans in the 1930s, for the British, there was a perceived *need*. Until the 1920s, the sprawling British Empire, upon which the sun never set, was well served by the unparalleled scale of British maritime power. With the emergence of practical international and intercontinental airline service, there was an obvious need to develop air routes to connect London with the Empire.

In fact, the name "Empire" was the appellation of what was arguably the most important series of flying boats produced in Britain. Manufactured by Short Brothers, the Empire also had the distinction of being one of the first aircraft ordered into production while still on the drawing board.

In 1933, British Imperial Airways head S.A. Dismore had convinced the British government that it could make the bold promise to carry mail throughout the Empire — or at least to southern Africa, India, Singapore and Australia — by air for surface postage rates. Known as the Empire Airmail Scheme, this plan led to a contract to establish such an airmail service, and British Imperial Airways placed its order with Short Brothers for 28 of the big, but untried, aircraft.

The first S.23 Empire class boat made its initial flight on July 4, 1936, and the Empire Airmail Scheme was officially inaugurated in June 1937 when 3,500 pounds of mail were delivered to South Africa.

The S.23 measured 88 feet in length, 31 feet 9.75 inches high, and had a wing span of 114 feet. It weighed 40,500 pounds fully loaded and fueled. The S.23 was powered by four Bristol Pegasus XC nine-cylinder radial engines, each rated at 920 horsepower, which in turn provided a cruising speed of 164 mph. It had a service ceiling of 20,000 feet, and its range was 760 miles. It carried a crew of five, accommodating 24 passengers. The S.23s were also known as "C-Class" flying boats, because each was given a name beginning with the letter "C." The first ship was *Canopus*.

British Imperial staged its flights through a hub at Alexandria in Egypt, with the S.23 known as *Clio* and *Calyp-*

so flying the mail to and from Southampton. An aircraft named *Centurion* served South Africa, while *Calypso* continued east to India and beyond. Meanwhile, the longer-range *Caledonia* was used to open service to New York by way of Newfoundland. In 1938, the *Cambria* was experimentally refuelled in flight as a means of extending its range.

British Imperial Airways (which became British Overseas Airways before World War II) took delivery of 28 Empire Class boats, and Australia's Qantas purchased three. There were 11 of the improved S.30 boats produced before the war. These were equipped with Bristol Perseus XIIc sleave-valve engines, which provided greater range. Powered by Bristol IV Hercules engines, the S.26 "G-Class" boats had the longest range of the Empire flying boats, and were intended specifically for the North Atlantic.

During World War II, several Empire flying boats were commandeered by the Royal Air Force, but most continued with British Overseas Airways, flying the dangerous air routes between Britain and Gibraltar, through the Mediterranean and into Asia.

Many of the Empire flying boats would remain in service until 1947.

RIGHT: LAUNCHED IN 1936, CANOPUS WAS THE FIRST SHORT S.23 EMPIRE FLYING BOAT. BELOW: THE G.26 GOLDEN HIND WAS ONE OF THE "G-CLASS" LONG RANGE EMPIRE BOATS DEVELOPED FOR THE NORTH ATLANTIC. IT SERVED WITH THE RAF IN THE WAR, AND WITH HARTY FERRY FROM 1947 TO 1954.

THE SHORT/MAYO COMPOSITE

The idea of extending the range of the Empire flying boats, especially on the high-profile North Atlantic route, was constantly on the minds of the staff of British Imperial Airways. In 1937, the airline's technical general manager, R.H. Mayo, came up with the unique idea of piggybacking a smaller flying boat onto the back of a modified Short S.23, thus creating the strange Short/Mayo Composite aircraft.

The Composite operated under the theory that an aircraft can carry a heavier load — in fuel and payload — than that with which it can take off. Therefore, the idea was for the S.21 *Maia* (a redesigned S.23) flying boat to lift the

S.20 *Mercury* to altitude, launch it, and return to base while it continued across the Atlantic.

The S.20 *Mercury* was 51 feet in length, 20 feet 3 inches high, and had a wing span of 73 feet. It had a normal gross weight of 12,500 pounds, and 20,500 pounds for composite operations. The S.20 was powered by four Napier Rapier V 16-cylinder radial engines, each rated at 340 horsepower. This gave it a cruising speed of 180 mph at 10,000 feet, and air-launching gave it a range of 3,900 miles with a 1,000-pound payload. The S.21 *Maia* was 84 feet 11 inches in length, 32 feet 7.5 inches high, and had a wing

span of 114 feet. It had a normal gross weight of 38,000 pounds, but 27,700 pounds for composite operations. The S.21 was powered by four Bristol Pegasus XC nine cylinder radial engines, each rated at 920 horsepower. This provided a cruising speed of 165 mph at 5,000 feet. It had a service ceiling of 20,000 feet, and its range was 850 miles.

The first combined flight took place in January 1938, and the first Transatlantic flight came on July 20. On October 6-7, 1938, a 6,045-mile flight from Dundee in Scotland, across two continents to Cape Town in South Africa, was completed in 42 hours.

ABOVE: *MAIA* AND *MERCURY* WERE AN ODD COUPLE, BUT R.H. MAYO'S IDEA WORKED. HAD IT NOT BEEN FOR WORLD WAR II, BRITISH IMPERIAL AIRWAYS WOULD HAVE BEEN ABLE TO EXPLOIT THEIR FULL POTENTIAL. THE TWO AIRCRAFT WERE COMMANDEERED BY THE ROYAL AIR FORCE, BUT THEY WERE OPERATED AS SEPARATE AIR-CRAFT. *MAIA* WAS DESTROYED IN A BOMBING RAID IN 1941, AND *MERCURY* WAS SCRAPPED.

THE DOUGLAS DOLPHIN

While the legendary lineage of commercial aircraft that were produced by the Douglas Aircraft Company can generally be said to have started with the DC-1, the first Douglas aircraft type to be used routinely as an airliner was a seaplane whose first flight preceded that of the DC-1 by three years.

Donald Douglas originally conceived this trim monoplane flying boat as personal transport, but it would eventually perform many roles. The idea was born in the heady days before the stock market crash of October 1929 brought down the curtain on the Roaring Twenties and ushered in the Great Depression.

Douglas was at least a year too late with the little craft that he called Sinbad. It took shape in Santa Monica, Cali-

fornia, during the winter of 1929-1930. The single prototype Sinbad airplane had a yacht-like aluminum hull and carried up to eight passengers in quiet comfort. Had it not been for the stock market crash, the Sinbad would have flown into the waiting arms of eager consumers. But times changed quickly that winter, and few people could afford such an airplane for private use.

The saviors of the production series of aircraft, which were called Dolphins, would be the United States military services, who found the Dolphin particularly suited to their needs. The US Coast Guard, US Navy and US Marine Corps purchased 23

RIGHT: **THE US ARMY AIR CORPS Y1C-12 AT SANTA MONICA IN DECEMBER 1931.** *BELOW:* **A COMMERCIAL DOLPHIN DURING A 1935 TOUR OF THE FAR EAST.** *OPPOSITE BOTTOM:* **A US COAST GUARD RD DOLPHIN IN THE HARBOR AT SAN PEDRO, CALIFORNIA.**

between them, under the RD (Transport, Douglas) designations. The US Army would eventually acquire two dozen under the C-21, C-26 and C-29 transport designations, some of which later bore the observation amphibian designations OA-3 and OA-4. One of these was intended for the private use of President Franklin Roosevelt. Although he did not actually fly in it, the aircraft was employed as a courier plane to bring packets to him when he was aboard his yacht or at remote locations.

Eventually, there were 58 production Dolphins manufactured, with one being sold to the Argentine Navy and 10 delivered to airlines, corporate customers and individuals. Among those who did buy Dolphins were the wealthy Vanderbilt family, the French billionaire Armand Esders, the Standard Oil Company and a gentleman from Seattle named William Edward Boeing. The founder of the rival Boeing Airplane Company had procured a Dolphin for his own personal use.

There were also a few airline customers, including Wilmington-Catalina Airlines of Southern California, and China National Aviation, which was a subsidiary of Pan American Airways.

The Dolphin was 43 feet 10 inches in length, 14 feet 1 inch high, and had a wing span of 60 feet. It had a gross weight of 9,387 pounds. The Dolphin was powered by a pair of radial engines, although the specific type varied from one aircraft to the next.

BELOW: THE DOLPHIN CONTINUED TO BE POPULAR DECADES AFTER IT WAS IN PRODUCTION. THIS AIRCRAFT IS THE DOLPHIN THAT WAS OWNED BY WILLIAM EDWARD BOEING FROM 1934 TO 1940. NICKNAMED ROVER BY BOEING, IT LATER SERVED WITH THE CATALINA CHANNEL AIR SERVICE IN CALIFORNIA. IN THE EARLY 1970S IT WAS ACQUIRED BY COLGATE DARDEN III IN SOUTH CAROLINA AND RESTORED AS IT IS SEEN HERE.

THE SIKORSKY S-42 CLIPPER

By the mid-1930s, Pan American Airways had built an extensive route structure in Latin America and the Caribbean, and was vigorously expanding its service elsewhere. The key area targeted for expansion was the Pacific. Larger aircraft would be needed. The Sikorsky S-40, which entered service on Pan Am Caribbean routes in 1930, was seen as a step in the right direction, but the airline asked the planemaker for something bigger. The result was the four-engine S-42, first sketched on the back of a menu during a conversation between Igor Sikorsky and Charles Lindbergh.

The S-42 first flew on March 30, 1934, and promptly set four weight-to-altitude records — several of them with Charles Lindbergh at the controls. The first of the legendary Pan Am "Clippers," all ten of the S-42s would be produced for that airline. They were 69 feet in length, 21 feet 9 inches high, and had a wing span of 118 feet 2 inches. Total wing area measured 1,340 square feet, while they

weighed 24,000 pounds empty, and had a gross weight of 42,000 pounds.

The S-42 was powered by four Pratt & Whitney Hornet radial engines, each rated at 750 horsepower. This gave the S-42 a top speed of 190 mph, and a stall speed of 65 mph. It had a service ceiling of 16,000 feet, and its range was 1,120 miles.

In April 1935, Pan American sent the first S-42, with Captain Ed Musick at the controls, on a survey flight of the Pacific. In service, the S-42s would be operated on Pan Am's Manila-Hong Kong route, as well as between Seattle and Alaska and between New York and Bermuda. An S-42 was also used to cut flight time between New York and Buenos Aires almost in half because it needed fewer stops.

RIGHT: THE INTERIOR OF AN S-42 LOOKING FORWARD TOWARD THE FLIGHT DECK FROM THE DINING COMPARTMENT. BELOW: FOUR POWERFUL HORNETS SNARL AS THIS PAN AMERICAN S-42 TAKES OFF. OPPOSITE BOTTOM: CAPTAIN ED MUSICK'S SIKORSKY S-42 AT THE PAN AMERICAN PIER IN MANILA HARBOR IN 1934.

THE LOCKHEED SIRIUS TINGMISSARTOQ

Perhaps the most famous seaplane conversion from an aircraft not normally used as a seaplane was the Lockheed Model 8 Sirius that was named *Tingmissartoq* — the Inuit word for "one who flies like a bird" — by a boy in Greenland. What made the moment of this naming particularly romantic was the fact that this particular Sirius was in Greenland as part of a historic flight by Charles Lindbergh and his wife, Anne Morrow Lindbergh. It was also the aircraft that was celebrated in Anne's best-selling book *North to the Orient*.

The Model 8 — itself called Sirius after the brightest star in the sky — was created by Jack Northrop when he was an engineer at Lockheed. Designed initially as a landplane, it made its first flight in 1929. With Lindbergh as the first customer, a dozen further orders were promptly forthcoming. The Model 8 was 27 feet 1 inch in length, 9 feet 3 inches high, and had a wing span of 42 feet 9.25 inches. It weighed 2,978 pounds empty, and had a gross weight of 4,600 pounds. The Sirius was powered by a Pratt & Whitney R-1340 Wasp radial engine rated at 450 horsepower. This provided the aircraft with a top speed of 185 mph, and a cruising speed of 150 mph. It had a service ceiling of 20,000 feet, and its range was 975 miles.

In 1931, with the aircraft retrofitted in seaplane configuration, Charles and Anne boarded their Sirius and made the flight to the Far East that would be described in *North to the Orient*. They island-hopped across the North Pacific to Japan through Alaska and the Aleutian chain, and traveled into China, evaluating potential airline routes. Damaged in Hankow, the Sirius was returned to Lockheed for rebuilding and installation of a 710-horsepower Wright SR-1839 Cyclone engine.

In July 1933, the legendary aviator and the best-selling author embarked on another airline survey flight. This time, the Lindberghs headed out across the stormy North

LEFT: **THE DISTINCTIVE BLACK AND ORANGE SIRIUS KNOWN AS *TINGMISSARTOQ* CARRIED CHARLES AND ANNE LINDBERGH ACROSS TWO OCEANS.**

Atlantic on the route that made Charles a household name in 1927. Indeed, the scope of this flight was far more ambitious than Lindbergh's legendary New York-to-Paris solo flight. Instead of simply crossing the Atlantic, he and his wife would set out to circumnavigate a sizable portion of it, looking at potential crossing routes in both the North Atlantic and the South Atlantic. It was during their refuelling stop in Angmagssalik, Greenland, on their outbound leg that *Tingmissartoq* got its name. Plane and crew continued through Europe to Moscow on their much-publicized tour. From Europe, the Sirius carried them south across Africa to Gambia, from which they crossed the South Atlantic to Brazil. *Tingmissartoq* appeared in the sky over New York on December 19, 1933, as the city turned out to welcome the Lindberghs. The aircraft, like its crew, had earned a place in history.

THE SUPERMARINE WALRUS

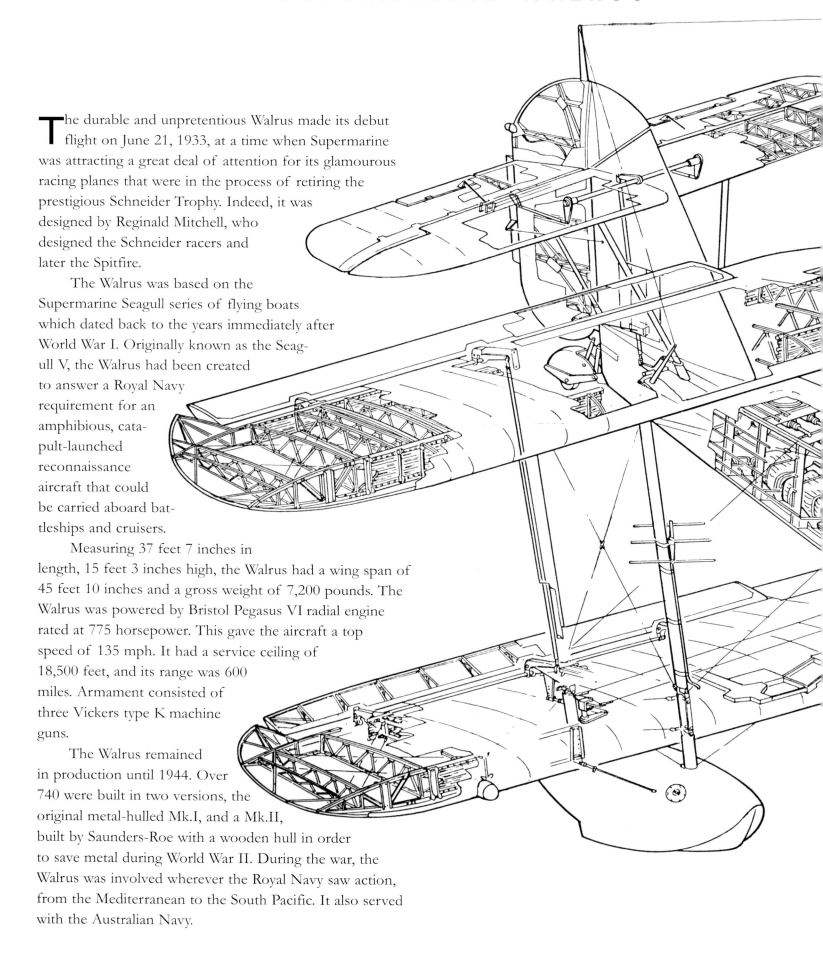

The durable and unpretentious Walrus made its debut flight on June 21, 1933, at a time when Supermarine was attracting a great deal of attention for its glamourous racing planes that were in the process of retiring the prestigious Schneider Trophy. Indeed, it was designed by Reginald Mitchell, who designed the Schneider racers and later the Spitfire.

The Walrus was based on the Supermarine Seagull series of flying boats which dated back to the years immediately after World War I. Originally known as the Seagull V, the Walrus had been created to answer a Royal Navy requirement for an amphibious, catapult-launched reconnaissance aircraft that could be carried aboard battleships and cruisers.

Measuring 37 feet 7 inches in length, 15 feet 3 inches high, the Walrus had a wing span of 45 feet 10 inches and a gross weight of 7,200 pounds. The Walrus was powered by Bristol Pegasus VI radial engine rated at 775 horsepower. This gave the aircraft a top speed of 135 mph. It had a service ceiling of 18,500 feet, and its range was 600 miles. Armament consisted of three Vickers type K machine guns.

The Walrus remained in production until 1944. Over 740 were built in two versions, the original metal-hulled Mk.I, and a Mk.II, built by Saunders-Roe with a wooden hull in order to save metal during World War II. During the war, the Walrus was involved wherever the Royal Navy saw action, from the Mediterranean to the South Pacific. It also served with the Australian Navy.

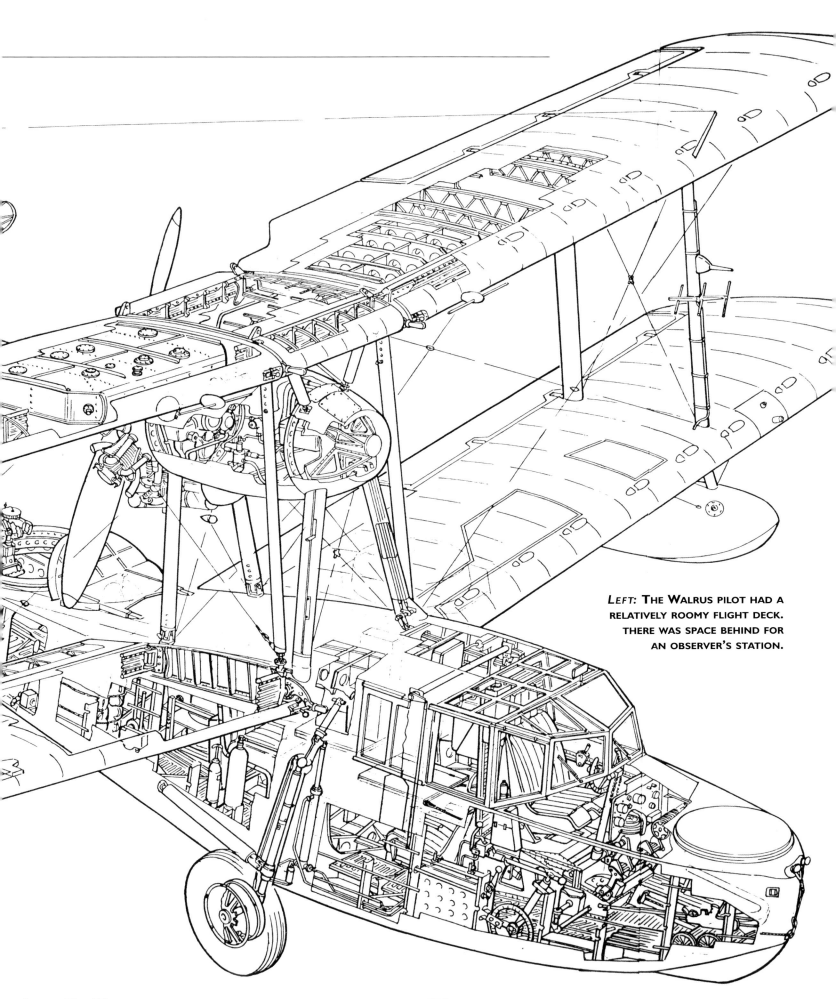

LEFT: **THE WALRUS** PILOT HAD A RELATIVELY ROOMY FLIGHT DECK. THERE WAS SPACE BEHIND FOR AN OBSERVER'S STATION.

ABOVE: **THE WALRUS** WAS AN AMPHIBIAN, WITH WHEELS THAT RETRACTED INTO THE LOWER WINGS. IN SHIPBOARD SERVICE, THE WHEELS WOULD GO FOR MANY TAKE-OFFS AND LANDINGS WITHOUT BEING USED.

THE CURTISS CONDOR

NR12384

Curtiss
Wright
CONDOR

BYRD ANTARCTIC EXPEDITION II
CURTISS WRIGHT CONDOR

BYRD ANTAR
EXPEDITI

RIGHT: **THE CONDORS USED BY RICHARD EVELYN BYRD'S 1940-1941
ANTARCTIC EXPEDITION WERE PAINTED IN THE CIVILIAN COLORS OF
AMERICAN AIRWAYS AND CARRIED CIVILIAN REGISTRATION.**

The last biplane airliner produced in the United States, the Curtiss T32 Condor first flew in 1933, at a time when the Boeing 247 and Douglas DC-series monoplanes were poised to revolutionize airline service worldwide. Nevertheless, the 12-passenger Condor was utilized by both Eastern Air Transport and with American Airways during the 1930s. In this role, the Condor flew as a land-plane, but in its most legendary role, it wore pontoons.

In addition to the commercial customers, who bought 45 aircraft between them, the US Army bought two Con-dors as C-30s, and the US Navy acquired two under the designation R4C-1. Originally earmarked for use by the US Marine Corps, they were used as part of the Antarctic expedition undertaken in 1940-1941 by retired admiral Richard Evelyn Byrd, head of the US Antarctic Service, and probably the foremost polar explorer active at the time.

Byrd had commanded the naval aviation unit of the Navy expedition to Greenland in 1919, and, in May 1926, he flew with Floyd Bennett from King's Bay, Spitsbergen to the North Pole and back. In 1928, Byrd made his first

Antarctic expedition and established his base, "Little America," on Ross Sound, which is still a major research center. He made the first flight over the South Pole in 1929, and returned several times, including 1934, when he spent an entire Antarctic winter there. In 1940, Byrd used the Condors for survey flights that resulted in the discovery of five new mountain ranges, a large peninsula, five islands, more than 100,000 square miles of area, and 700 miles of previously unexplored sections of Antarctic coastline.

The Curtiss T32 Condor was 48 feet 7 inches in length, 16 feet 4 inches high, and had a wing span of 82 feet. Weighing 17 pounds empty, it had a gross weight of pounds. A pair of Wright Cyclone nine-cylinder radial engines, each rated at 720 horsepower, gave the Condor a cruising speed of 167 mph. It had a service ceiling of 23,000 feet, and its range was 716 miles. By 1941, however, the Condor's days were over. The Army retired their last one in 1938, and the Navy did the same after the Antarctic expedition.

THE MARTIN M-130 CLIPPER

The importance of the role that was played by Pan American Airways (Panair) in the development of American airliners cannot be minimized. Their work on the great seaplane airliners of the 1930s was pivotal, and in the 1950s and 1960s, Pan American would be a defining and deciding factor in Boeing's development of both the 707 and 747 jetliners. Indeed, one might say that for three decades Panair was more important in the history of aircraft development than any other single airline in the world.

In 1934, the eyes of Pan American's visionary president, Juan Trippe, were on the Pacific. He realized the importance of "The Pacific Rim" many years before it was fashionable. His airline had launched Sikorsky's S-40 and S-42, but with the extreme long range routes in Pacific, he needed something more. The winning design was the M-130, produced by the Glenn L. Martin Company. First flown on December 30, 1934, the M-130 was 90 feet 10.5 inches in length, 24 feet 7 inches high, and had a wing span of 130 feet. It had a gross weight of 52,252 pounds. The M-130 was powered by four Pratt & Whitney R-1830 Twin Wasp 14-cylinder radial engines, each rated at 830 horsepower. This gave the aircraft a cruising speed of 157 mph. It had a service ceiling of 17,000 feet, and, most important, its range was 3,200 miles — long enough for the route across the Pacific that Trippe envisioned. He was to buy three of the planes at a cost of $430,000 each.

The route of the "Clippers," as Trippe's transocean seaplanes came to be known, would be across the center of the Pacific, rather than around the northern rim, using the Aleutian chain as stopping points. This route was laid out

RIGHT: THE *CHINA CLIPPER* FLIES PAST SAN FRANCISCO'S TELEGRAPH HILL EN ROUTE TO THE PACIFIC. THE UNDER-WING SPONSONS ("SEAWINGS") PROVIDED STABILITY IN THE WATER AND KEPT SPRAY AWAY FROM THE FUSELAGE DURING TAKE-OFF. *BELOW:* THE *CHINA CLIPPER* TREASURE ISLAND IN SAN FRANCISCO BAY. *OPPOSITE BOTTOM:* THE *PHILIPPINE CLIPPER* AT MIDWAY ISLAND.

in a series of legs, with the longest being the 2,210 miles from San Francisco to Honolulu. The rest of the crossing to Manila and Hong Kong would involve stops at the islands of Midway, Wake and Guam. Because there were no facilities or tourist accommodations for passengers on these islands, Pan American not only constructed mooring docks for the seaplanes, but also built, shipped and installed prefabricated hotels, complete with dining rooms and bathrooms for each room.

In March 1936, Pan American took delivery of its three M-130s, which were dubbed *Hawaii Clipper, Philippine Clipper* and *China Clipper*. In November, the latter aircraft became the first Martin Clipper to complete a passenger-carrying flight to Manila.

The M-130 carried 41 passengers on shorter flights and 14 on the longest transpacific runs where maximum fuel had to be carried. On night flights, seats could be folded to provide 18 berths for sleepy passengers. In addition

to sleeping arrangements, there was a galley on board and a comfortable lounge where passengers could relax with a card game or conversation. These luxurious features were modeled after the Pullman service offered by the railroads at the time, and were much better than the amenities offered to passengers by most commercial airlines since the 1950s.

World War II would abruptly end Pan American Clipper service in the Pacific, but both *China Clipper* and *Philippine Clipper* had each completed 10,000 flying hours when they were commandeered for military service in 1942. *Hawaii Clipper* (later renamed *Hawaiian Clipper*) disappeared in July 1938 on a flight from Guam to Manila. The reasons for its loss have never been determined, but evidence has been cited that would suggest that she may have been hijacked by Japanese agents.

RIGHT: A RARE COLOR PHOTOGRAPH OF THE *CHINA CLIPPER* ON SAN FRANCISCO BAY. *BELOW:* A MARTIN M-130 OVER THE UNFINISHED GOLDEN GATE BRIDGE IN JANUARY 1936. *OPPOSITE BOTTOM:* THE LOUNGE ABOARD THE M-130 AFFORDED ROOM TO RELAX, AND A WAITER TO PROVIDE BEVERAGES.

THE BOEING 314 CLIPPER

The biggest and grandest of the Pan American Clippers was the Boeing Model 314. It was the first commercial flying boat to be produced by the Seattle company since 1929, but it was also the last Boeing seaplane to go into production.

In 1936, with the Martin M-130s already in service on the Pacific routes, Pan American solicited bids for an even larger flying boat, stipulating that the craft had to be capable of carrying 10,000 pounds of payload for 2,400 miles at an altitude of 10,000 feet. Both Martin and Sikorsky submitted proposals, but Boeing won the order for six of the new boats, basing their Clipper on their experience with the XB-15, which was, at the time, the largest landplane bomber to have been produced. In fact, it was larger than either the B-17 or B-29 bombers that Boeing would produce during World War II.

The 314 measured 106 feet in length, 27 feet 7 inches high, and had a wing span of 152 feet. The total wing area was 2,480 square feet. It had a gross weight of 84,000

pounds — greater than any production aircraft ever built except the Dornier Do.X. The 314 was powered by four Wright GR-2600 Double Cyclone 14-cylinder radial engines, each rated at 1,600 horsepower. This provided the 314 with a cruising speed of 183 mph. It had a service ceiling of 13,400 feet, and its range was 4,200 miles.

The first flight occurred on June 7, 1938, while the first 314, dubbed *Yankee Clipper*, was delivered to Pan American in January 1939. In March, the big ship undertook a survey flight to Europe, in anticipation of regularly-scheduled service. As the world's largest airliner, the *Yankee Clipper* attracted a great deal of attention. She carried a crew of ten, and had plush

RIGHT: PAN AMERICAN'S *DIXIE CLIPPER* UNLOADING PASSENGERS AFTER A TRANSATLANTIC VOYAGE. *BELOW:* THE LAST BOEING 314A TAKES OFF FROM THE WATERS OF ELLIOT BAY. THE SEATTLE SKYLINE CAN BE SEEN IN THE BACKGROUND. *OPPOSITE BOTTOM:* ENJOYING LUNCH IN THE DINING AREA OF A BOEING 314.

seats in nine compartments on two decks for up to 74 pas- sengers. For night flights, there were 36 berths, or 38 if convertible seats were installed in the central lounge area. There were even dressing rooms.

Regular service on the New York to Marseilles via Lis- bon route began in June 1939 via the *Dixie Clipper*. A month later, the *Yankee Clipper* started routine flights to Southampton. Based on the initial success of the 314 on its Atlantic route — and despite the beginning of World War II in September — Pan American ordered an additional six aircraft under the designation 314A. The major difference between

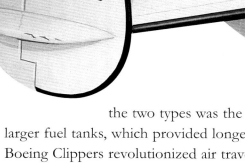

the two types was the 314A's larger fuel tanks, which provided longer range. The Boeing Clippers revolutionized air travel, and had it not been for World War II, they would have had a long and glorious career. It is a great tribute to the aircraft and the people who developed it that the Clipper made such an impact in so short a time.

Of the six 314As, only three were delivered to Pan American. The others were deliv- ered to British Overseas Airways (BOAC), and were taken over by the British

government. One was assigned as Prime Minister Winston Churchill's personal transport. When the United States entered the war, the American Clippers were taken over by the Navy and USAAF, but continued to be flown by Pan American crews. One of these was used by President Franklin Roosevelt.

After the war, Pan American briefly resumed service with the 314s on both the Atlantic and Pacif- ic, but the last transocean flight was in January 1946. Flights between Hawaii and San Francisco Bay would contin- ue until April. Wartime advances in landplane technology had rendered the 314s obsolete, so Pan Am sold the Clippers to World Airways, who used them on Caribbean routes until the early 1950s, at which time they were scrapped.

ABOVE: **THE 314'S LOUNGE/DINING AREA WAS AMID-SHIP ABOVE THE SPONSONS, WHICH WERE HYDROSTABILIZERS DESIGNED TO PROVIDE BALANCE IN THE WATER AND BETTER HIGH-SPEED TAXIING. SEATING AND BERTH AREAS WERE ON THE LOWER DECK, WITH BAGGAGE AND FREIGHT CARRIED ON THE TOP. THE CREW QUARTERS WERE IN THE NOSE AND BETWEEN THE BAGGAGE AREAS. THE PASSENGER CABINS COULD BE RECONFIGURED FOR MORE SEATING OR MORE SEATING SPACE.**

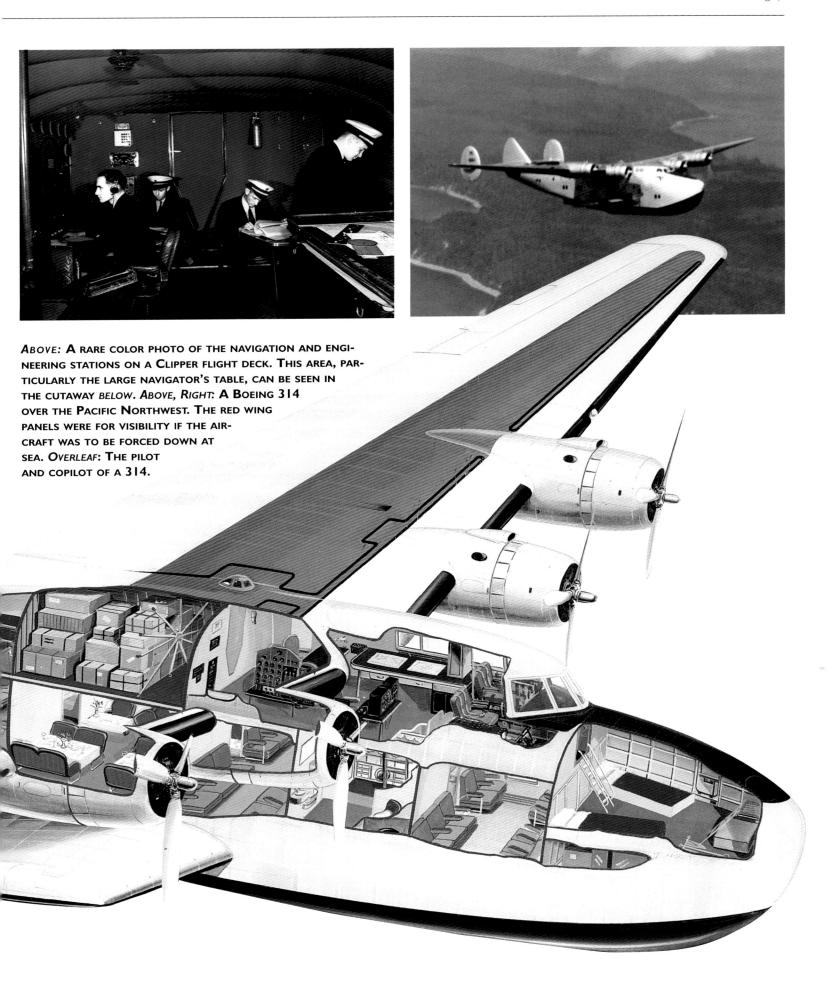

ABOVE: A RARE COLOR PHOTO OF THE NAVIGATION AND ENGI-
NEERING STATIONS ON A CLIPPER FLIGHT DECK. THIS AREA, PAR-
TICULARLY THE LARGE NAVIGATOR'S TABLE, CAN BE SEEN IN
THE CUTAWAY *BELOW*. *ABOVE, RIGHT*: A BOEING 314
OVER THE PACIFIC NORTHWEST. THE RED WING
PANELS WERE FOR VISIBILITY IF THE AIR-
CRAFT WAS TO BE FORCED DOWN AT
SEA. *OVERLEAF*: THE PILOT
AND COPILOT OF A 314.

THE HEINKEL HE.115

ABOVE: IN OPERATIONS OVER THE NORTH SEA AND IN THE ARCTIC, THE HEINKEL HE.115 PROVED ITSELF DURABLE AND RELIABLE. DESIGNED AS A TORPEDO BOMBER, ITS MOST FAMOUS ACTIVITIES INVOLVED ITS USE IN CLANDESTINE OPERATIONS.

Though the firm Ernst Heinkel Flugzeug Werke is best known for its He.111 medium bomber, produced in large numbers during World War II, the company produced several other important aircraft, including the He.177 /277 heavy bomber, the He.219 night fighter, the He.162 jet fighter and the He.115 — an Axis patrol bomber that is perhaps best remembered as an Allied spy plane!

Heinkel began development of the He.115 in 1935 in response to a request for proposals issued by the *Reichsluft-fahtministerium* (German Air Ministry) for a twin-engine, tor-pedo-carrying floatplane. The resulting aircraft, with its broad wing and pencil-thin fuselage, made its first flight in August 1937. Pre-production aircraft were delivered to the Luftwaffe in 1938, but at a slow rate because of budgetary reasons. This led Heinkel to solicit additional orders outside Germany.

With their long, rugged coastlines, Denmark, Norway and Sweden found such a potentially reliable floatplane to be attractive, and deliveries began in the summer of 1939. Ironically, within a year, Germany would attack Denmark and Norway, and He.115s would be found on opposite sides.

When Germany conquered Norway in May 1940, four of the Norwegian He.115s managed to escape to Scotland, where they were repaired and refurbished. Two of these were, in turn, painted in Luftwaffe markings and assigned to clandestine operations. One was based at Woodhaven, near Dundee in Scotland, and was used to fly secret agents into remote fjords on the coast of Norway. Such missions proved dangerous — not in Norway, but when the German-identified plane returned to the British coast — so operations were suspended.

In October 1941, the second Norwegian He.115 was sent to Malta, where it was flown by Lieutenant Haakon Offerdahl on numerous secret missions against the Germans in North Africa. On one occasion, Offerdahl landed in Tripoli harbor under the noses of the Germans and extracted two secret agents in broad daylight.

In service with the Luftwaffe, He.115s were used for mine-laying operations from Norway to the English Channel, and as a torpedo bomber in attacks on convoys headed from Britain to the Russian port of Murmansk. In one particular attack in July 1942, He.115s successfully sank 23 out of 36 ships in a convoy after the convoy scattered in the mistaken belief that the vessels were being hunted by German warships.

The He.115 developed a reputation for being a sturdy aircraft and one that was reliable in operations involving

landings and take-offs in high seas. Nevertheless, by 1944, it was determined that the aircraft was too slow and vulnerable for torpedo attacks, and it was thus withdrawn from service.

The He.115C-1 was 56 feet 9 inches in length, 21 feet 7.75 inches high, and had a wing span of 73 feet 1 inch. The total wing area was 933.23 square feet. It weighed 15,146 pounds fully equipped. When unfueled and without payload, the craft had a gross weight of 23,545 pounds.

The He.115C-1 was powered by a pair of BMW 132K nine-cylinder radial engines, each rated at 960 horsepower at sea level, and 830 at 2,800 feet. This gave the aircraft a top speed of 180 mph at sea level, and a cruising speed of 174 mph at 3,280 feet. It had a service ceiling of 16,950 feet, and its maximum range was 1,740 miles. North Sea operations often utilized the full range.

THE CONSOLIDATED PBY CATALINA

The Catalina was produced in larger numbers than any other flying boat during World War II, and probably in larger numbers than any flying boat in history. A total of 3,281 were built — 2,159 by Consolidated in San Diego, California; 369 by Vickers/Canadair in Montreal; 362 by Boeing of Canada in Vancouver, British Columbia; 235 by Consolidated in New Orleans; and 155 by the Naval Aircraft Factory in Philadelphia. The original prototype was the last aircraft built by Consolidated in Buffalo, New York before the move to California.

Ordered by the US Navy in 1933 under the designation XP3Y-1, the new aircraft was designed by Isaac "Mac" Laddon and bore a clear resemblance to the earlier Consolidated P2Y Ranger and its predecessors, which Laddon had also designed. It first flew on March 21, 1935, with Bill Wheatly at the controls and Mac Laddon at his side.

In June, the Navy placed an order for 60 aircraft under the PBY patrol bomber designation (the "Y" was the Navy's designation for Consolidated). This order was instrumental in Consolidated's move to San Diego. Company president Reuben Fleet didn't want to build seaplanes in a place where the water was frozen part of the year.

The first production PBY-1 was launched on October 5, 1936 in the bay where Glenn Curtiss had made the first American hydroplane flight 25 years earlier. Meanwhile, Consolidated had received a Navy order for 60 additional PBY-2s, and the factory was enlarged. This boosted production area to 543,000 square feet, including an enclosed paved yard where overflow final assembly operations could be conducted in the California sunshine.

While the future would find the Catalina in service with the US Navy, as well as many other navies and air forces from Britain to the Soviet Union, there were also commercial versions that carried the boat's name into the Arctic and around the world. It was in service with Britain's Royal Air Force Coastal Command in 1939 that the PBY first used the given name "Catalina," by which it would eventually be known in US Navy as well.

The first of these was built in 1937 for Dr. Richard Archbold, leader of an American Museum of Natural His-

RIGHT: THIS IMAGE OF **PBY**s ON THE **C**ONSOLIDATED ASSEMBLY LINE IN **S**AN **D**IEGO IS A REMINDER THAT IT WAS THE MOST SUCCESSFUL SEAPLANE IN **A**MERICAN HISTORY.

BELOW: **D**R. **R**ICHARD **A**RCHBOLD AND HIS TEAM SITTING ON THE WING OF THE **C**ATALINA KNOWN AS *GUBA,* PARKED AT THE SHORE OF **L**AKE **H**ABBEMA, **N**EW **G**UINEA, 11,000 FEET ABOVE SEA LEVEL. THE *GUBA* WAS A KEY PART OF THE 1938 **A**MERICAN **M**USEUM OF **N**ATURAL **H**ISTORY EXPEDITION TO THE **N**ETHERLANDS **E**AST **I**NDIES.

tory expedition to the Netherlands East Indies (now Indonesia), specifically New Guinea. He named it *Guba*, a Motu word meaning "sudden storm." Archbold left San Diego June 24 on the first transcontinental flight ever staged with a flying boat. He landed in New York 17 hours, 3.5 minutes later. In August, Archbold agreed to sell the first *Guba* to the Russian government, which had retained Sir Hubert Wilkins, the British explorer, to head the search for Soviet aviator Sigismund Levanesky, who was missing, along with his crew, after an attempted transpolar flight.

A replacement *Guba* was delivered to Archbold, and the transpacific flight started from San Diego on June 2, 1938. Archbold flew to Pearl Harbor in 18 hours, 3 minutes; then hopped to Wake Island on June 6, and on June 9-10 made a passage through unflown skies to Hollandia, New Guinea. During the next 11 months, *Guba* made 168 flights and carried more than 280 tons of supplies to expedition field camps in the interior. Many of the landings were on Lake Habbema, located 200 miles inland and 11,000 feet above sea level. Archbold reported that the Catalina "enabled us to do in 10 minutes work which could not have been done in two years had we used the available means of land transportation."

When the New Guinea work was nearing an end, the Australian and British governments enlisted Archbold's participation in a survey of an air route across the Indian Ocean, which had never been flown. *Guba* left Hollandia on May 12, 1939 for Sydney, then flew nonstop across Australia on June 3. Heading homeward, *Guba* crossed Africa in two hops, setting down on Lake Victoria and on the Congo River. On June 29-30, it made an over-water flight of 3,190 miles from Dakar to St. Thomas in the West Indies in 19 hours and 33 minutes.

When *Guba* landed in New York, Archbold and his crew were whisked off to the Aviation Building at the World's Fair for an official welcome. *Guba* returned to San Diego Bay on July 6, completing the first round-the-world flight ever made by a seaplane and the first made by any aircraft at the globe's greatest diameter.

Less than two months later, World War II began in Europe, and Consolidated received contracts from France

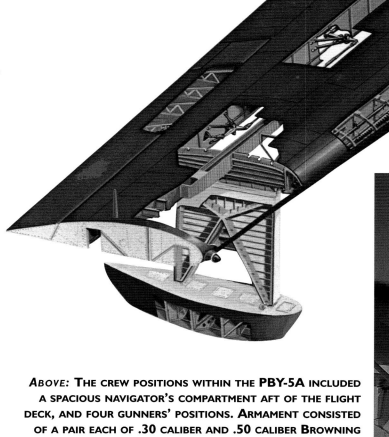

ABOVE: **THE CREW POSITIONS WITHIN THE PBY-5A INCLUDED A SPACIOUS NAVIGATOR'S COMPARTMENT AFT OF THE FLIGHT DECK, AND FOUR GUNNERS' POSITIONS. ARMAMENT CONSISTED OF A PAIR EACH OF .30 CALIBER AND .50 CALIBER BROWNING MACHINE GUNS.**

RIGHT: **A DETAIL VIEW OF A PRESERVED US NAVY PBY-5A SHOWING THE FLIGHT DECK AND FORWARD OBSERVER'S POSITION. ONE MACHINE GUN WAS INSTALLED HERE.**

BELOW: **THE INTERNAL STRUCTURE OF THE PBY-5A, SHOWING DETAILS OF CONSTRUCTION. NOTE THE RETRACTABLE WING-TIP PONTOONS AND RETRACTABLE LANDING GEAR.**

and Britain for large quantities of Catalinas. In December, the US Navy ordered 200 PBY-5s at a cost of just over $20 million, the largest contract for airplanes ever awarded by the US government.

The PBY-5 differed from earlier Catalinas in that it had retractable tricycle landing gear. The PBY-5 was also the definitive version, with over half the total production run being US consisting of PBY-5s, PBY-5As or equivalent export versions.

The Catalina would play a pivotal role in World War II. It was a Royal Air Force Coastal Command Catalina that found the German battleship *Bismarck* 550 miles west of Land's End on May 26, 1941, some 24 hours after she had eluded a Royal Navy surface force. Word of the sighting was passed to the air-sea task force that was to finally sink the mighty *Bismarck* on May 27.

A US Navy PBY found itself in combat a few minutes after sunrise December 7, 1941, when this patrolling Catalina sighted the periscope of a Japanese midget submarine off the entrance to Pearl Harbor. It was at 6:33 that the pilot, Lieutenant William P. Tanner, dropped smoke pots to mark the spot, and a few minutes later the destroyer USS *Ward* attacked and sank the sub. Within the hour, Japanese bombers were attacking Pearl Harbor and the United States was at war.

When General Douglas MacArthur was forced to leave the Philippines in the face of the Japanese onslaught, it was a PBY that carried him part of the way to Australia. When the tide finally turned for the Americans with victory in the naval Battle of Midway in June 1942, it was a Catalina that gave advance warning of the Japanese battle fleet, and Lieutenant W. L. Richards led four PBYs in a courageous torpedo attack.

At Midway, the main enemy force was discovered June 4 by Lieutenants Howard Ady and William Chase, who were piloting a PBY-5 search plane. They sent repeated messages giving distance and bearing, then managed to elude planes launched against them by four Japanese carriers. After the Battle of Midway had been won, PBYs rescued 27 downed pilots.

Indeed, in every theater of operations, the Catalina became celebrated as a rescue craft. In February 1942, as the Japanese were invading the East Indies, a Dutch Catalina went to the aid of the crew of a sinking freighter that had been attacked by Japanese planes. Amazingly, the Catalina managed to squeeze all 87 sailors aboard!

The USAAF also used Catalinas under the OA-10 observation amphibian designation. These were deployed in North Africa as bombers and in the Pacific for air-sea rescue missions. By early 1943, OA-10s, PBYs and other rescue Catalinas were operating throughout the Pacific Theater to retrieve stranded Allied pilots from hostile waters and shores, often within range of enemy gunfire. Nicknamed "Dumbo" (after Walt Disney's flying elephant), they were credited with bringing back more than 160 flight crewmen in their first 18 months — a figure that would significantly increase by the end of the war. In October 1943, three PBYs operating from the Sepik River managed to evacuate 219 Australian soldiers and 12 tons of equipment from the heart of the New Guinea jungle.

While the Pacific PBYs performed their innumerable missions in the long campaign from Guadalcanal to Okinawa, Catalinas in the Atlantic were chiefly occupied with anti-submarine warfare. This began with the organization of the Neutrality Patrol, continued through the period of "measures short of war" (the United States was not then officially in the war), and reached a climax in the 1942-1943 offensives against the German U-boat menace.

All Catalina models had the same overall dimensions, except height, which ranged from 18 feet 6 inches in the prototype to 22 feet 4 inches in the PBY-6A, the final type, introduced in 1944. The ubiquitous PBY-5 was 63 feet 10 inches in length, 18 feet 11 inches high, and had a wing span of 104 feet. The total wing area was 1,400 square feet. It weighed 17,400 pounds empty, and had a gross weight of 26,200 pounds. The PBY-5A weighed 20,910 pounds empty, and had a gross weight of 33,975 pounds. The PBY-5 was powered by a pair of Pratt & Whitney R-1830-82 engines, each rated at 1,200 horsepower for take-off and

RIGHT: **THE PBY-6A** WAS CHARACTER-
IZED BY THE LARGE RADAR INSTALLATION
LOCATED ABOVE THE FUSELAGE AFT OF
THE FLIGHT DECK. *BELOW:* **A PBY-5** IN
LATE 1942-VINTAGE **US** NAVY MARKINGS
LIFTS CRISPLY FROM THE WATER ON TAKE-
OFF. *OPPOSITE BOTTOM:* NOTE THE ANTEN-
NA WIRES TRAILING FROM THE WINGS OF
THIS ROYAL AIR FORCE CATALINA MK. IV.

1,050 at 5,700 feet. This gave the aircraft a top speed of 200 mph at 5,700 feet, and a cruising speed of 189 mph at sea level. The PBY-5A's R-1830-92 had a similar rating.

The PBY-5 had a service ceiling of 17,700 feet, and its range was 2,860 miles on patrol or 2,645 miles with 2,000 pounds of bombs. The PBY-5A had a service ceiling of 14,700 feet, and its range was 2,545 miles on patrol or 1,820 miles with 2,000 pounds of bombs.

The last PBY, a PBY-6A, retired from the US Navy in 1957, but Catalinas had a commercial career that would extend from before World War II to the twenty-first century. American Export Airlines operated three as early as 1939, and the Australian airline Qantas had them in scheduled service in the South Pacific from 1944 to 1958. Other airlines in the region — including Cathay Pacific, KLM, Thai Airways and Trans-Australian — also bought surplus

PBYs after the war and used them on scheduled routes until the 1960s.

In the Caribbean, Catalinas were operated by Air France and Bahamasair, while Aeroservices Parrague used them on the route between Chile and Easter Island. Jacques Cousteau, the famous filmmaker and oceanographer, employed a PBY-6A Catalina called *Flying Calypso* — his ship was named *Calypso* — until it was lost in a fatal crash in July 1979.

In the 1980s and 1990s, roughly 100 surviving Catalinas continued to serve on the air show circuit or as fire bombers. Long-term preservation of these aircraft will be aided by the fact that they operate primarily from freshwater lakes, where the danger of serious corrosion is quite a bit less than it was when the aircraft operated in a salt water environment.

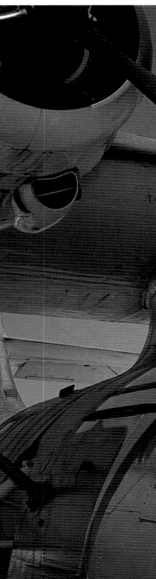

RIGHT: **THE CIVILIAN CATALINA** *POLAR CAT,* **CIRCA 1964.** *BELOW:* **A VIEW OF A RESTORED CATALINA IN 1943 VINTAGE US NAVY MARKINGS, AS PHOTOGRAPHED IN 1993.** *OPPOSITE BOTTOM:* **JACQUES COUSTEAU'S** *FLYING CALYPSO,* **CIRCA 1976, AND THE HV FLYING SERVICE** *SUPER CAT,* **CIRCA 1974.**

THE CONSOLIDATED PB2Y CORONADO

When the Consolidated XPB2Y-1 made its debut flight on December 17, 1937, with Bill Wheatly and George Newman at the controls, it was the largest flying boat in the US Navy. It was also the first to be conceived as a "flagship" aircraft, i.e. as one that would carry the admiral in command of the Aircraft Scouting Force.

The production PB2Y-2s, which were not ordered until 1939, had a larger hull than the prototype — hence the increase in gross weight from 49,754 pounds to 60,441 pounds. When the United States entered World War II, US Navy deliveries were behind schedule, and planned deliveries of Coronados to Britain were also delayed. The British are credited with giving it the name "Coronado" (after the island in San Diego Harbor visible from the Consolidated plant), as they had given the PBY its name, "Catalina."

The principal production version was the PB2Y-3, of which 210 were built, with 10 going to the British as Coronado Mk. I. The British aircraft were used as transatlantic transports, and over 30 of the US Navy's PB2Ys were converted by Rohr Aircraft as 44-passenger transports. The PB2Y-3 measured 79 feet 3 inches in length, 27 feet 6 inches high, and had a wing span of 115 feet. The total wing area was 1,780 square feet. It weighed 41,031 pounds empty, and had a gross weight of 68,000 pounds.

The PB2Y-3 was powered by four Pratt & Whitney R-1830-88 Twin Wasp radial engines, each rated at 1,200 horsepower on take-off and 1,000 horsepower at 19,500 feet. This gave the aircraft a top speed of 224 mph at 19,500 feet, and a cruising speed of 140 mph. With a service ceiling of 20,900 feet, it had a ferry range of 3,120 miles, or 1,380 miles with 8,000 pounds of payload.

Many of the PB2Y-3s, both transports and patrol bombers, were later retrofitted with R-1830-92 engines and provisions for rocket-assisted take-off, and redesignated as PB2Y-5. Several of these were used as 22-stretcher hospital planes on such missions as the evacuation of seriously wounded troops from the Philippines and Iwo Jima.

All of the US Navy's Coronados were retired before the end of 1945, and nearly all were scrapped immediately, a sad commentary on a slow but capable heavy-lifter.

RIGHT: ONLY SIX PB2Y-2S WERE BUILT, AND THEY WERE USED FOR THE PROJECT BAKER INSTRUMENT LANDING EXPERIMENTS. *BELOW:* AN EARLY PB2Y-3 CUTS POWERFULLY THROUGH THE WAVES ON TAKEOFF. *OPPOSITE BOTTOM:* A PB2Y-5 PATROL BOMBER EQUIPPED WITH THE LARGE ASV RADAR FAIRING AFT OF THE FLIGHT DECK.

THE ARADO AR.196

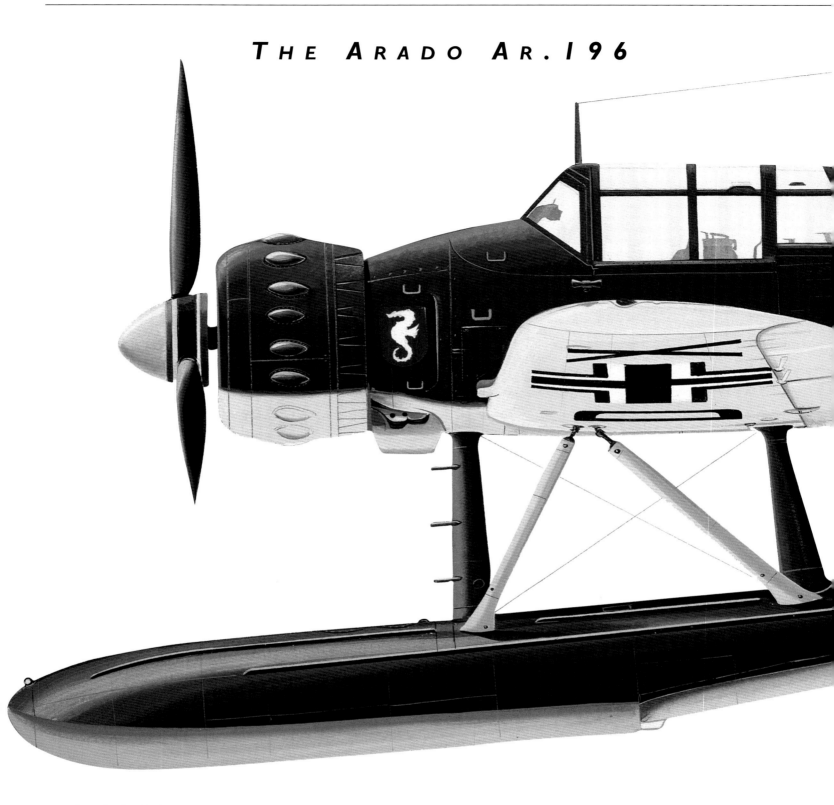

The plucky little Arado Ar.196 was conceived as a ship-board scouting aircraft, but experienced its finest hour as a fighter-interceptor! It evolved from the earlier, albeit similar Ar.95 and Ar. 195 biplane floatplanes. When it was designed in 1936, the Ar.196 was considered innovative for its being a monoplane, and it was selected for production over the Focke-Wulf Fw.62, with which it was in competition for an order from the German Kriegsmarine (Navy). Based at Aalborg, Denmark as part of a coastal reconnaissance unit, the Ar.196 became operational with the Kriegsmarine in May 1940. Meanwhile, Ar.196s were also being assigned to duty aboard the Kriegsmarine's heavy warships.

Ar.196s received assignments to the great battleship *Bismarck* prior to its fateful cruise into the Atlantic in May 1941. They were launched to attack Royal Air Force Coastal Command Catalina flying boats that were reporting the *Bismarck's* location to Royal Navy warships.

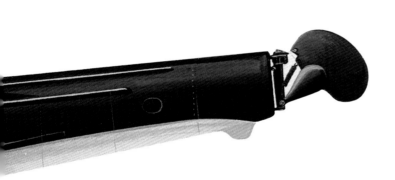

LEFT: FIRST DELIVERED IN NOVEMBER 1939, THE ARADO AR.196A-2 SERIES WAS THE SECOND PRODUCTION BLOCK AND THE FIRST TO BE EQUIPPED WITH TWO 20MM FORWARD-FIRING CANNONS AND THE 7.9MM MACHINE GUN AT THE REAR OF THE COCKPIT.

After the *Bismarck* was sunk, the Kriegsmarine chose to keep its major surface ships in port and to rely on U-boats to wage war against Allied shipping. The Ar.196 found a role in this strategy, being assigned to provide air cover for the U-boats at their most vulnerable position: when they were entering or exiting their ports on the Bay of Biscay and western France. The Ar.196s proved to be an effective interceptor, fending off the cumbersome Whitleys that were sent to hunt U-boats.

Also in 1941, Ar.196s were briefly assigned to a unit operating on the Black Sea from Constanza, Romania, but these were soon transferred to the Aegean Sea area. By 1944, there were four Ar.196 squadrons operating in the eastern Mediterranean, but these were eventually reassigned to the Eastern Front.

The definitive aircraft of the series was the Ar.196A-3, which was 35 feet 11.5 inches in length, 14 feet 7 inches high, and had a wing span of 40 feet 9.75 inches. The total wing area was measured 304.6 square feet. It weighed 5,148 pounds empty, and had a gross weight of 7,282 pounds. The Ar.196 was powered by a BMW 132K nine-cylinder radial engine rated at 960 horsepower. This provided the aircraft with a top speed of 194 mph at 3,280 feet, and a cruising speed of 166 mph. It had a service ceiling of 22,965 feet, and its range was 497 miles.

THE DORNIER DO.24

The illustrious Dornier Do.24 was part of the lineage of flying boats that included the equally important Do.X and Do.J Wal. As with those aircraft, an important part of the Do.24's history involved license production outside Germany. Whereas the earlier Dorniers were manufactured in Italy and the Netherlands to avoid the Treaty of Versailles limitations on aircraft production within Germany, the Do.24 was manufactured abroad simply because in the beginning there was more interest in the Netherlands than there was at home.

The Do.24 originated with the Netherlands *Marine Luchtvaartdienst* (Naval Air Ministry), who sought a successor to the Wals which had been produced through 1931 in the Netherlands by Aviolanda. The *Marine Luchtvaartdienst* liked the Wal but wanted something newer and larger with the same pedigree.

Designed specifically for the *Marine Luchtvaartdienst,* the first Do.24 was built in Germany and made its initial flight on Lake Constance on July 3, 1937. It was powered by three Wright R-1820-1852 Cyclone engines rather than German engines, because the United States government

had just released them for export to the Netherlands and they were preferred by the *Marine Luchtvaartdienst.*

Production Do.24s were to be built in the Netherlands by Aviolanda and De Schelde. However, those firms were unable to handle the orders immediately; therefore some were built in Switzerland. Deliveries of 60 aircraft to the *Marine Luchtvaartdienst* were complete by early 1939, and production began in the Netherlands on 48 improved Do.24K aircraft with bigger Cyclone engines. Many of these and earlier aircraft were shipped to the Netherlands East Indies (now Indonesia) for use by the Netherlands Navy as patrol aircraft.

German interest in the Do.24 languished until April 1940, when the two original prototypes — still parked at the Dornier plant — were pressed into service during the invasion

RIGHT: **THE FIRST NETHERLANDS-BUILT DO.24K WAS DESTINED FOR SERVICE WITH THE NETHERLANDS NAVY.**
BELOW: **A SOMEWHAT DRAMATIC PHOTOGRAPH OF THE FOURTH DO.24 CASUALLY RIDING IN 10-FOOT SWELLS.**
OPPOSITE BOTTOM: **THE DORNIER-BUILT FOURTH DO.24 WAS THE SECOND PRODUCTION SERIES AIRCRAFT.**

13,120 feet. This gave the Do.24T a top speed of 206 mph at 8,530 feet, and a maximum endurance cruising speed of 155 mph. It had a service ceiling of 34,605 feet, and its maximum range was 2,920 miles.

By the end of 1942, Do.24Ts were equipping air-sea rescue units along every part of German-occupied coastline, from Norway to Greece, and additional Do.24Ts were supplied to non-combatant but pro-Axis Spain for air-sea rescue. Meanwhile, the Netherlands Navy had survived German occupation in the East Indies; however, when the Japanese invaded in December 1941, Do.24s were used to launch a counterstrike. Despite performing admirably against Japanese ships, they were forced to retreat to Australia when the Japanese finally overran the Netherlands colony. Four surviving aircraft were turned over to the Royal Australian Air Force, while one was used by the Netherlands Intelligence Service for secret missions until October 1943. In Luftwaffe service, the aircraft continued in the air-sea rescue role until the end of the war. In March 1943, they were also used in the final evacuation of German forces from the Crimea, with the last flight out carrying 40 persons.

Ultimately, over 300 of the durable Do.24s were built, making it the penultimate German-designed flying boat, second only to the Dornier Wal in numbers produced. Several Luftwaffe Do.24s survived the war — despite their vulnerability to Allied fighters during their rescue missions — but these were scrapped. However, the Do.24s supplied to Spain continued to be operational until the 1970s.

of Norway. They performed admirably under fire, flying troops in and out of fjords in the far north. A month later, Germany conquered the Netherlands, and German troops captured the Aviolanda and De Schelde factories, where 23 Do.24Ks remained in various states of completion.

By this time, the Luftwaffe had rethought the Do.24, placing it in the context of their pressing need for an air-sea rescue aircraft; Aviolanda and De Schelde were in turn ordered to continue production. They were now producing aircraft for the German invader that had been designed in Germany to begin with. Subsequent German procurement included retrofitting German instruments and larger rescue hatches were provided at a convenient level for use by a person in a life raft.

When Wright Cyclone engines ran out, further aircraft were produced with German engines. Built in France as well as the Netherlands, these were the definitive Do.24T versions, which were 72 feet 4 inches in length, 18 feet 10.4 inches high, and had a wing span of 88 feet 7 inches. The total wing area comprised 1,162.5 square feet. The Do.24T weighed 20,723 pounds empty, and had a gross weight of 35,715 pounds. It was powered by three BMW-Bramo 323R-2 Fafnir nine-cylinder radial engines, each rated at 1,000 horsepower for take-off and 940 horsepower at

ABOVE: A Do.24T IN THE GREEN CAMOUFLAGE LIVERY COMMON TO LUFTWAFFE AIRCRAFT IN THE 1942-1944 PERIOD. *RIGHT:* MAINTENANCE WORK BEING DONE ON A Do.24 TAIL TURRET. *OPPOSITE:* THE FIRST Do.24K. THIS SERIES WERE CALLED "X-BOATS" BECAUSE THEY ALL HAD REGISTRATION NUMBERS BEGINNING WITH "X." *BELOW:* A SPANISH SEARCH AND RESCUE Do.24, CIRCA 1954.

THE DORNIER DO.26

While most large German aircraft developed in the late 1930s were combat aircraft disguised as long-range airliners, the Dornier Do.26 actually evolved from an airline requirement for a long-range airliner. Like its first cousin, the Do.24, the Do.26 was inspired by the Dornier Wal, which had been impressive for its long career of Atlantic crossings in an era before Atlantic crossings were routine.

In 1936, Deutsche Luft Hansa (later Lufthansa) announced that it was in the market for an aircraft capable of routine flights from Lisbon to New York. The Dornier design, with its innovative cantilever wing, was chosen, and the Do.26 prototype, known as *Seeadler* (*Sea Eagle*), made its first flight on May 21, 1938. The second prototype began regular service in the spring of 1939 — not on the North Atlantic route, but across the South Atlantic, where the Wal had proven its mettle a decade before. The first flight was a dramatic 12,800-mile round trip earthquake relief mission to Chile.

As it was with many promising flying boat airliners of the era, the promising career of the Do.26 was interrupted by the beginning of World War II, which compelled an end to Atlantic flights.

The Do.26s then in production as eight-passenger airliners were completed as military reconnaissance aircraft, and they were commandeered by the Luftwaffe and placed into service during the invasion of Norway in the spring of 1940. Their range allowed them to handle with ease the distances involved in flights into even the northern-most fjords.

However, two of the five Do.26s committed to the campaign were intercepted by Royal Air Force Hurricane fighters on May 28, as they were airlifting mountain troops to Rombaksfjord. One was shot down and the other captured after a forced landing. The remaining Do.26s were withdrawn and ulti-

mately retired without having served the illustrious career enjoyed by the Do.24.

The Do.26 measured 80 feet 8.5 inches in length, 22 feet 5.75 inches high, and had a wing span of 98 feet 5 inches. The total wing area was 1,291.67 square feet. It weighed 24,912 pounds empty, and had a gross weight of 49,600 pounds. The Do.26 was powered by four Junkers Jumo 205D six-cylinder, vertical-opposed-piston, compression ignition, two-stroke engines, each rated at 880 takeoff horsepower. This allowed the Do.26 a top speed of 201 mph at 8,530 feet, and a long-distance cruising speed of 160 mph. It had a service ceiling of 14,760 feet, and its maximum range was 4,410 miles.

RIGHT: THE FIRST DO.26, KNOWN AS
SEEADLER, DURING INITIAL DEUTSCHE
LUFT HANSA EVALUATION ACTIVITIES IN
MAY 1938. *BELOW*: A SLEEK *SEEADLER*
IN LUFTWAFFE MARKINGS MAKES A HIGH-
SPEED TAKEOFF, BOUND FOR NORWAY IN
THE SPRING OF 1940.

BELOW: **THE DORNIER DO.26** WAS THE SLEEKEST AND AERODYNAMICALLY CLEANEST FLYING BOAT TO BE DEVELOPED IN THE FIRST HALF OF THE TWENTIETH CENTURY. ITS NARROW FUSELAGE AND CANTILEVER WING MADE IT LOOK FAST, BUT ITS MOST IMPRESSIVE PERFORMANCE FEATURE WAS ITS VERY LONG RANGE.

LEFT: THOUGH IT WAS DESIGNED FOR DEUTSCHE LUFT HANSA, THE DO.26 IS BEST REMEMBERED FOR WEARING THE "SPLINTER CAMOUFLAGE" WARPAINT OF THE DEUTSCHE LUFTWAFFE. IN LOOKING AT ITS CLEAN LINES AND THE PROVISION MADE FOR A BOW TURRET, ONE WONDERS IF A COMBAT ROLE WAS NOT IN THE PLANNING AT DORNIER FROM THE BEGINNING. THE PROMINENT BOW TURRET CARRIED A SINGLE MG.151 20MM CANNON. IN ADDITION, THERE WERE 7.9MM MACHINE GUNS MOUNTED IN FIXED POSITIONS AT THE "WAIST" AND ANOTHER AFT-FIRING 7.9MM GUN IN A WATER-TIGHT MOUNT UNDER THE TAIL.

BELOW: SEEN HERE WEARING THE LUFTHANSA REGISTRATION P5+DH, THE FIRST DO.26 WAS DELIVERED TO DEUTSCHE LUFT HANSA IN 1937 AS THE *SEEADLER.* HAD WORLD WAR II NOT INTERVENED, *SEEADLER* AND HER SISTER SHIPS WOULD HAVE EARNED THEIR LIVELIHOOD COMPETING WITH PAN AMERICAN'S BOEING 314 CLIPPERS ON THE NORTH ATLANTIC ROUTE. FOR ALL ITS TRIM STYLISHNESS, HOWEVER, THE DO.26 CARRIED LESS THAN A QUARTER OF THE PASSENGERS ACCOMMODATED BY A CLIPPER.

THE BLOHM UND VOSS BV.138

The Bv.138 was the first flying boat built by Hamburger Flugzeugwerke, a subsidiary of the Blohm und Voss shipbuilding firm. Though it made its first flight in 1937, it dated back to design studies done in 1934. While the Dornier Do.24 and Do.26 flying boats, with which the Bv.138 would serve, had roots in commercial aircraft, the Bv.138 was designed from the beginning to be a military reconnaissance aircraft.

The project suffered long delays in the early stages of development because the hull of the prototype was prone to excessive drag in the water. Flight testing of early production aircraft finally got under way in April 1940 — coincidentally at the same time that German forces were invading Norway and Denmark. The need for a seaplane to support these operations led to the Bv.138A being pressed into service after an abbreviated evaluation.

Problems encountered with engines and propellers led to an extensive redesign program, a new engine and ultimately the definitive version, the Bv.138C. A total of 227 would be produced by the end of 1943.

The Bv.138C was the same size as the Bv.138A: 65 feet 1.5 inches in length, 19 feet 4.25 inches high. With a wing span of 88 feet 4.25 inches, the total wing area of the Bv.138C was 1,205.6 square feet. It weighed 25,948 pounds empty, and had a gross weight of 38,912 pounds.

The Bv.138C was powered by three Junkers Jumo 205D six-cylinder, vertical-opposed-piston, compression ignition, two-stroke engines, each rated at 880 takeoff horsepower. This

gave the aircraft a top speed of 177 mph at sea level, and a cruising speed of 146 mph at 3,280 feet. It had a service ceiling of 16,400 feet, its range was 2,670 miles, and its typical mission endurance was 6.5 hours.

Bv.138Cs entered squadron service with the Luftwaffe in the spring of 1941, and were assigned to units in France for North Atlantic operations and in Norway for missions over the North Sea, where they shadowed and helped in the attack of convoys bound for the Soviet Union. After 1943, they were also deployed to the Mediterranean, but

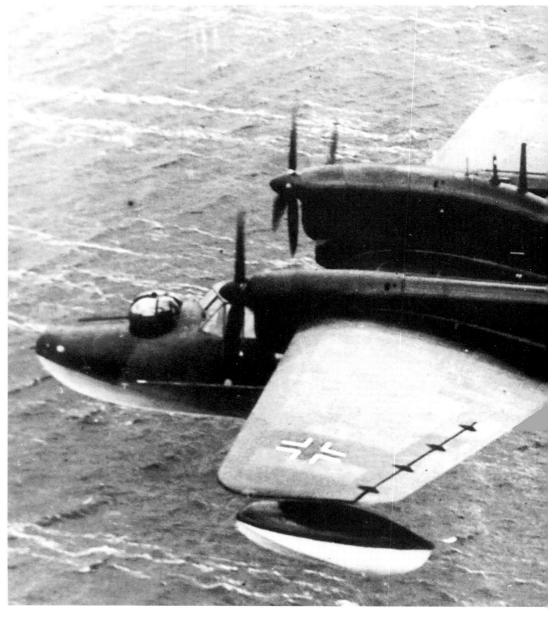

their primary role through the end of the war would be in operations against Allied convoys.

The Bv.138 was armed with a bow turret carrying a 13mm MG.131 machine gun in its nose turret, and a second fixed gun aft of the wing. Thus armed, Bv.138s actually engaged in air-to-air combat with Allied flying boats and even fighters. In the autumn of 1941 off Norway, for example, Bv.138s are known to have shot down a Beaufighter and a Catalina. Even when they failed to score a kill, the durable Bv.138s were hard to shoot down and they often limped home despite severe damage. In one case, a Bv.138 was mauled by Royal Air Force Hurricanes for 90 minutes, but survived.

The Luftwaffe Bv.138s had a symbiotic relationship with the Kriegsmarine's U-boats. They were the eyes of the underwater fleet, tracking their targets, but they were also supported by the submarine force. Long-range operations were made possible by the innovative procedure of refuelling the Bv.138s at sea from U-boats.

By the summer of 1943, Bv.138s were operating deep into the Soviet Arctic. A little-known secret German base was set up on the coast well inside Soviet territory. From this outpost, the sturdy seaplanes conducted missions as far east as the Yamal Peninsula, a thousand miles east of Moscow, and at least as far north. As such, they probably operated deeper inside enemy territory than any other German unit.

A Bv.138 was involved in what was possibly the last high-priority mission flown by the Luftwaffe during World War II. On May 1, 1945, Oberleutnant Wolfgang Klemusch was ordered to fly from Copenhagen to Berlin, which was, by that time, surrounded and besieged by the Soviet Red Army. Klemusch got through to Berlin, landed on a lake, and was met by the two couriers about whom he'd been told. They had their "special parcel," but they didn't have any proper identification. Klemusch rejected them and — unbeknownst to him — Adolf Hitler's will. He then kicked them out of his plane, loaded in 10 wounded soldiers, and flew safely back to Copenhagen.

BELOW: A LUFTWAFFE BV.138C ON PATROL OVER THE CHOPPY NORTH ATLANTIC.

THE GRUMMAN DUCK

Between the time it was founded by Leroy Grumman in 1929 and its merger with Northrop in 1994, the Grumman Aircraft Corporation produced more aircraft of different types for the US Navy than any other planemaker. Based at Bethpage, Long Island, New York, the "Iron Works," as Grumman was known, is best remembered for its line of "carrier cats." These were aircraft carrier-based fighters named for cats, which served the US Fleet from World War II to the Gulf War. They included the F4F Wildcat, F6F Hellcat, F8F Bearcat, F9F Panther and the F-14 Tomcat.

Grumman was also known for its family of seaplanes named for aquatic birds. Among these were the JF and J2F Duck, which served with the Fleet during World War II. The first Ducks, the JF-1 and JF-2, began their service with the US Navy and US Coast Guard in 1933. The "J" stood for "Utility" and the "F" was Grumman's company designation. Relatively few JFs were produced before the Duck was redesigned with an enclosed cockpit and redesignated

as J2F. These aircraft appeared in 1937, and about 100 were in service at the time the United States entered World War II. In 1942, Grumman was producing the J2F-5 and J2F-6 variants, of which 144 and 330 were built, respectively. The J2F-6 Duck was 34 feet in length, 15 feet 1 inch high, had a wing span of 39 feet and a gross weight of 6,711 pounds. It was powered by a Wright R-1820-54 Cyclone nine-cylinder, air-cooled, radial engine, rated at 900 horsepower. This gave the Duck a top speed of 190 mph. It had a service ceiling of 27,000 feet, and its range was 780 miles.

During the war, Ducks served as scouting and photographic planes, as well as for air-sea rescue and as target tugs.

RIGHT: A J2F-4 IN THE BLUE CAMOUFLAGE MARKINGS ADOPTED BY THE US NAVY IN 1942. BELOW: A BEAUTIFULLY RESTORED J2F-6 DUCK. THE HEAVY-DUTY LANDING GEAR THAT RETRACTED INTO THE CONTOURED FLOAT MADE THE DUCK A VERSATILE AMPHIBIAN. OPPOSITE BOTTOM: A J2F-4 IN PREWAR US NAVY MARKINGS, CIRCA 1940.

THE KAWANISHI H8K

Aside from the remarkable Mitsubishi "Zero," the aircraft produced by Japan during World War II are often overlooked in general surveys of the military aircraft of the period. One of the best candidates for an exception to this practice is the Kawanishi H8K, which is generally recognized as the best four-engine flying boat of the war in terms of performance and hydrodynamic characteristics.

The H8K appeared in 1940, having been designed as a longer-range replacement for the H6K flying boat, which was based on the Consolidated boats of a decade earlier. The H8K entered service in 1941. Its first combat mission was the largely forgotten, and unsuccessful, *second* attack on Pearl Harbor. In March 1942, three H8Ks took off from Watji in the Marshall Islands, and, refuelling from a submarine positioned en route, they flew over 2,000 miles to Hawaii, only to find impenetrable cloud cover. They turned back undetected, leaving a page of history unturned.

The H8K served extensively on long-range patrols and bombing missions in the Southwest Pacific, where it was given the Allied reporting name "Emily" under the convention that assigned Anglo-Saxon female names to Japanese bombers, and male names to fighters. The definitive Emily, the H8K2, entered service in 1943. It was heavily armored and heavily armed, with five 20mm cannons and a 7.7mm machine gun located in three powered turrets and fixed positions. It also carried eight 550-pound bombs or two 1,746-pound torpedoes.

The H8K2 measured 92 feet 3.5 inches in length, 30 feet high, and had a wing span of 124 feet 8 inches. The total wing area was 1,722.23 square feet. Weighing 40,520 pounds empty with a gross weight of 54,013 pounds, it was powered by four Mitsubishi Kasai 22 14-cylinder, air-cooled radial engines, each rated at 1,850 horsepower. This provided the H8K2 with a top speed of 290 mph at 16,400 feet and a cruising speed of 184 mph at 13,120 feet. It had a service ceiling of 28,740 feet, and its range was 3,800 to 4,447 miles, depending on payload, configuration and fuel.

A transport variant, the H8K2-L Seiku (Clear Sky), was put into service in 1943. It had less armament than the patrol bomber version, but it had the capacity to transport between 29 and 64 passengers. The transports accounted for 36 of the 167 H8K2s built.

Production of the H8K2, and work on an improved H8K3, continued until early 1945, when the government ordered the industry to concentrate on fighter production.

RIGHT: THE POWERED TURRETS OF THIS
H8K BEACHED AT MAKIN ISLAND WERE
USED BY JAPANESE TROOPS AS A STA-
TIONARY GUN POSITION UNTIL THEY
WERE KNOCKED OUT BY AMERICAN
TROOPS. *BELOW:* THE POWERED TURRETS
AND THE YAGI SEARCH RADAR ANTENNAE
CAN BE SEEN IN THIS VIEW OF A TAXIING
H8K2. *OPPOSITE BOTTOM:* AN H8K EMILY
IS SHOT DOWN OVER THE PACIFIC.

THE SHORT S.25 SUNDERLAND

Just as the Short Brothers Empire Class flying boats made a significant impact on British commercial aviation in the 1930s, the Short Sunderland flying boat turned out to be one of the most important British military aircraft of World War II.

Aside from its extended nose, the Sunderland was in fact quite similar to the Empire flying boats. It made its first flight in October 1937, and by the beginning of World War II in September 1939, a number of Sunderland Mk.Is were in service with the Royal Air Force Coastal Command, not only over the waters around Britain, but from the British base at Singapore as well.

During the war, Sunderlands participated in coastal patrols, air-sea rescue and anti-submarine operations. The first U-boat kill came in January 1940, and was to be the first of many. The effectiveness of the Sunderland as a U-boat hunter increased dramatically with the introduction of Torpex depth bombs in 1943. At the same time, Sunderlands were earning a reputation from German fighter pilots as an aircraft able to sustain severe punishment. They came to nickname the big boat *"Stachelschwein"* (Porcupine).

In addition to operations from bases in Britain, Sunderlands were also active in the Indian Ocean and in the Southwest Pacific with the Royal Australian Air Force.

There were a total of 721 Sunderlands produced, culminating with 143 Mk.Vs, which made their appearance in 1943. The Mk.V would continue in production until June 1946, a year after the end of the war in Europe, and Sunderlands remained in service with the Royal Air Force until 1959.

The Sunderlands were 85 feet 3.5 inches in length, 34 feet 6 inches high, and had a wing span of 112 feet 9.5 inches. The total wing area measured 1,687 square feet. The Sunderland Mk.V weighed 36,900 pounds empty, and had a gross weight of 60,000 pounds. The Sunderland Mk.I was powered by four Bristol Pegasus XXII nine-cylinder air-cooled, radial engines, each rated at 1,010 horsepower.

The Sunderland Mk.V was powered by four Pratt & Whitney Twin Wasp 14-cylinder radials, each rated at 1,200 horsepower. This gave the Mk.V a top speed of 213 mph at 5,000 feet, and a cruising speed of 133 mph at 2,000 feet. It had a service ceiling of 17,900 feet, and its range was 2,690 miles with a bomb load of 1,668 pounds.

ABOVE: **A RESTORED SHORT SUNDERLAND MK.V ON DISPLAY. THE MK.V WAS THE ULTIMATE SUNDERLAND.**

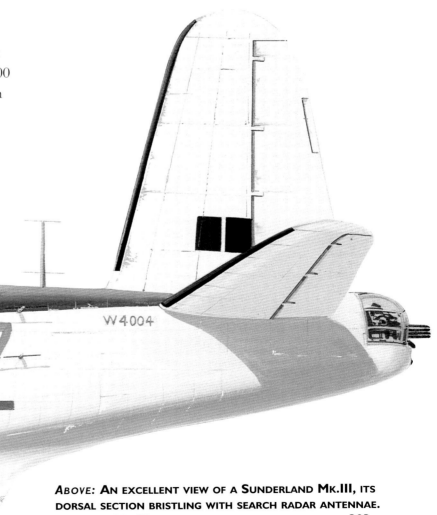

ABOVE: **AN EXCELLENT VIEW OF A SUNDERLAND MK.III, ITS DORSAL SECTION BRISTLING WITH SEARCH RADAR ANTENNAE. WITH THE MK.III, THE TOP TURRET, WITH ITS PAIR OF .303 CALIBER MACHINE GUNS, BECAME STANDARD EQUIPMENT ON ALL SUNDERLAND MODELS. THE MK.III FIRST FLEW IN JUNE 1942 AND WAS IN SERVICE WITHIN MONTHS. BEGINNING WITH THE MK.II AND INCLUDING THE MK.III, THE OVERALL GREEN AND BROWN CAMOUFLAGE OF EARLIER DAYS WAS REPLACED BY THE MOSTLY MILK-WHITE COLORING.**

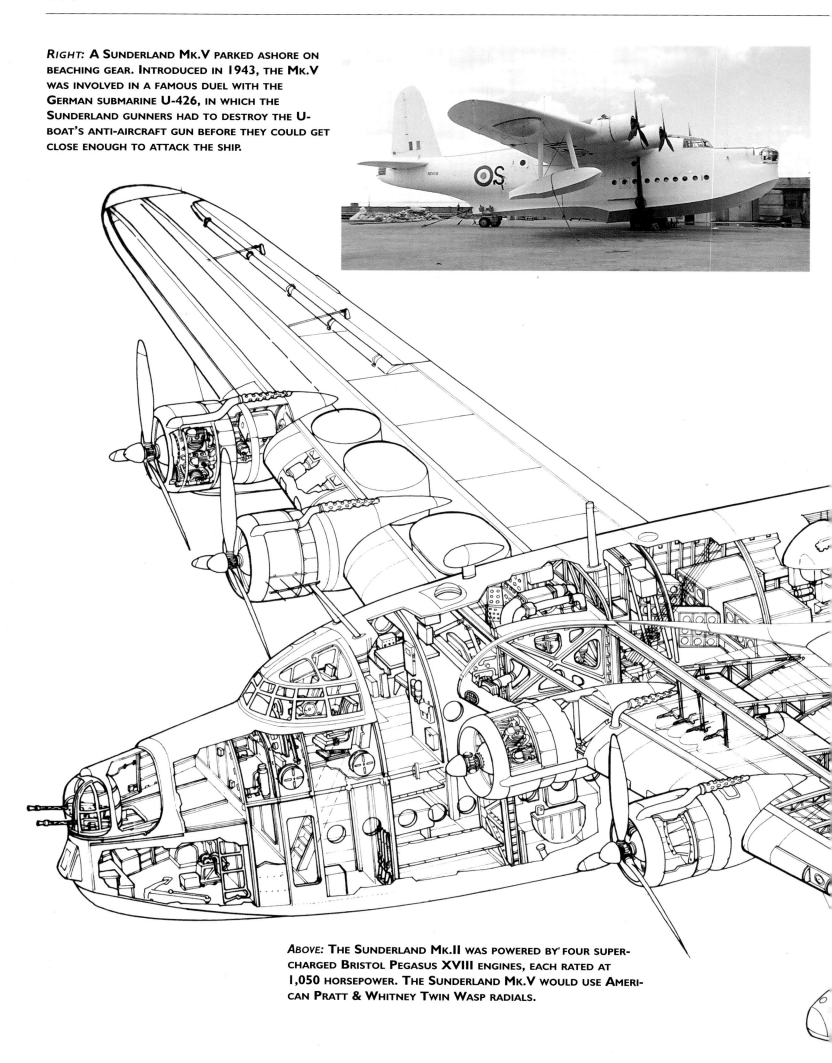

RIGHT: A SUNDERLAND MK.V PARKED ASHORE ON BEACHING GEAR. INTRODUCED IN 1943, THE MK.V WAS INVOLVED IN A FAMOUS DUEL WITH THE GERMAN SUBMARINE U-426, IN WHICH THE SUNDERLAND GUNNERS HAD TO DESTROY THE U-BOAT'S ANTI-AIRCRAFT GUN BEFORE THEY COULD GET CLOSE ENOUGH TO ATTACK THE SHIP.

ABOVE: THE SUNDERLAND MK.II WAS POWERED BY FOUR SUPER-CHARGED BRISTOL PEGASUS XVIII ENGINES, EACH RATED AT 1,050 HORSEPOWER. THE SUNDERLAND MK.V WOULD USE AMERICAN PRATT & WHITNEY TWIN WASP RADIALS.

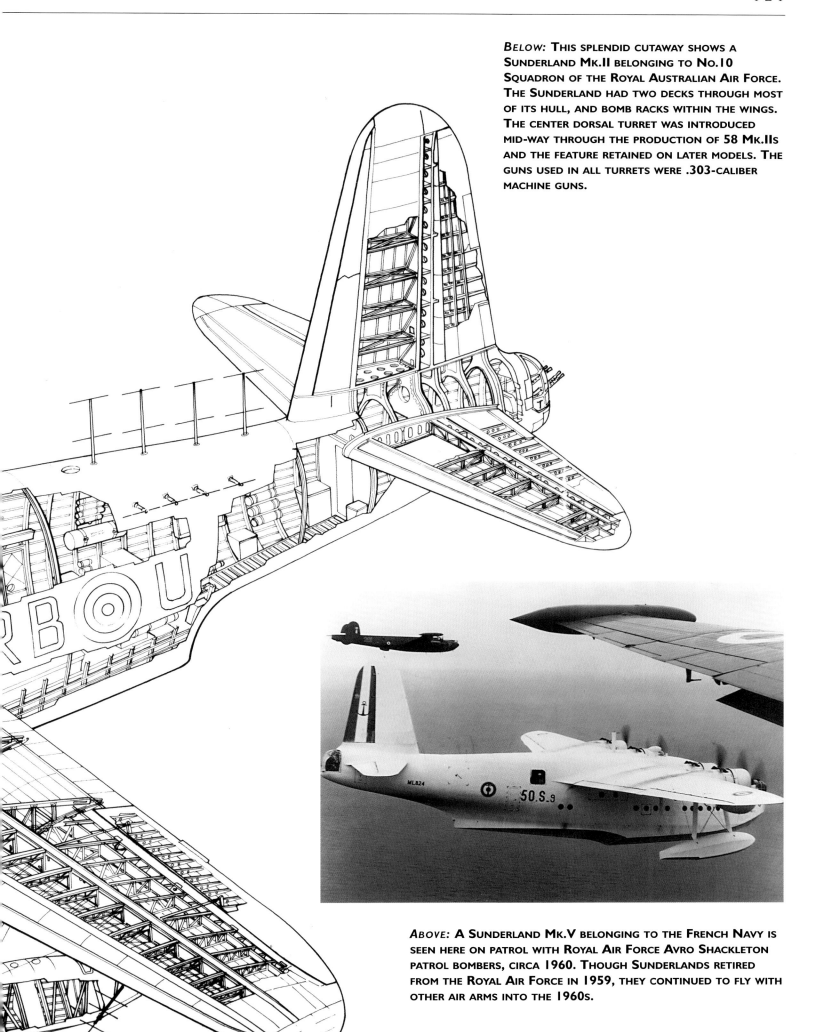

BELOW: THIS SPLENDID CUTAWAY SHOWS A SUNDERLAND MK.II BELONGING TO NO.10 SQUADRON OF THE ROYAL AUSTRALIAN AIR FORCE. THE SUNDERLAND HAD TWO DECKS THROUGH MOST OF ITS HULL, AND BOMB RACKS WITHIN THE WINGS. THE CENTER DORSAL TURRET WAS INTRODUCED MID-WAY THROUGH THE PRODUCTION OF 58 MK.IIs AND THE FEATURE RETAINED ON LATER MODELS. THE GUNS USED IN ALL TURRETS WERE .303-CALIBER MACHINE GUNS.

ABOVE: A SUNDERLAND MK.V BELONGING TO THE FRENCH NAVY IS SEEN HERE ON PATROL WITH ROYAL AIR FORCE AVRO SHACKLETON PATROL BOMBERS, CIRCA 1960. THOUGH SUNDERLANDS RETIRED FROM THE ROYAL AIR FORCE IN 1959, THEY CONTINUED TO FLY WITH OTHER AIR ARMS INTO THE 1960s.

THE SHORT S.25V SANDRINGHAM

After the success of the Short Sunderland as a wartime, long-range patrol bomber, it was obvious to Short Brothers that a version of it should be proposed as a post-war commercial transport. Anxious to reopen the old Empire flying boat routes interrupted by the war, British Overseas Airways Company (BOAC) agreed with the proposal. The first Sandringham Mk.I, a direct conversion of a Sunderland Mk.V, made its debut in November 1945, only two months after the end of World War II.

The Sandringham was 86 feet 3 inches in length, 22 feet 10.5 inches high, with a wing span of 112 feet 9.5 inches, the latter measurement being the same as the Sunderland. It had a gross weight of 56,000 pounds, and was powered by four Pratt & Whitney Twin Wasp 14-cylinder radials (also the same as the Sunderland), each rated at 1,200 horsepower. Weighing less and having the same power plant as the Sunderland, the Sandringham had a higher cruising speed; 221 mph. The Sandringham had a service ceiling of 21,300 feet. Its range was 2,410 miles.

The Sandringham could accommodate 22 passengers in seats, or 16 in its sleeper-convertible configuration. BOAC would take delivery of nine Sandringham Mk.Vs,

and five 37-seat Sandringham Mk.VIs were sold to airlines in Scandinavia, including SAS and DNL. Many of these aircraft continued in service into the 1980s, with second and third generation customers such as Antilles Air Boats and Ansett Australian.

The Short S.45 Solent was a similar commercial aircraft that was derived from the Short Seaford, a wartime flying boat that was originally designated Sunderland Mk.IV. Virtually the same size as the Sandringham, the Solent had a higher gross weight and could accommodate up to 44 passengers. It was powered by four Bristol Hercules 637 14-cylinder radials, each rated at 1,690 horsepower.

BOAC bought 12 Solents for use on its London to Cape Town route. They served only from 1948 to 1950, however, before being replaced by landplanes.

RIGHT: THE ANTILLES AIR BOATS
SANDRINGHAM KNOWN AS SOUTHERN
CROSS RIDING AT ANCHOR. *BELOW:* A
NICELY-MAINTAINED, FRENCH-REGISTERED
SANDRINGHAM, CIRCA 1963. *OPPOSITE
BOTTOM:* THE SHORT SOLENT CAN BE
DISTINGUISHED FROM THE SANDRINGHAM
BY THE SWEEP OF THE TAIL WHERE IT
INTERSECTS THE FUSELAGE.

THE MARTIN MARS

Many milestones in the history of aircraft development were reached during World War II, and one of them belongs to the gargantuan Martin Mars. The Mars had the distinction of being the largest flying boat produced to date and the largest American aircraft to be built prior to the Hughes Hercules (*"Spruce Goose"*).

The Mars measured 117 feet 3 inches in length, 38 feet 5 inches high, and had a wing span of 200 feet. The total wing area was 3,683 square feet. Weighing 75,573 pounds empty, it had a gross weight of 144,000 pounds and was powered by four Wright R-3350-18 Duplex Cyclone 18-cylinder air-cooled radial engines, each rated at 2,200 horsepower. This gave the Mars a top speed of 221 mph at 4,500 feet, and a cruising speed of 149 mph. It had a service ceiling of 14,600 feet, and its maximum range was 4,945 miles.

The big boat was originally ordered by the US Navy in 1938 as a patrol bomber under the designation XPB2M-1. The prototype was finished in November 1941, but an accidental fire spoiled plans for an elaborate launching ceremony and the first flight was delayed until July 1942. This big boat had two decks and a crew of 11.

In 1943, without having flown a single combat mission, the prototype had its powered turrets removed, and it was converted into a transport. No further patrol bomber Mars were built, but the US Navy ordered 20 Mars transports under the designation JRM-1. None of these were completed before the end of the war, however, and the order was cut to five. These aircraft differed from the patrol bomber in that they had a single rather than a double tail. The sixth and final Mars built, *Caroline Mars*, used the massive 28-cylinder 3000-horsepower Pratt & Whitney R-4360 engine, almost doubling the payload. It was designated JRM-2.

The JRM Mars fleet continued to serve throughout the 1950s on long transport routes, especially across the Pacific Ocean. When retired by the US Navy in 1956, they went to Flying Tankers Limited in Canada, where they served as fire-bombers for more than four decades.

RIGHT: FLIGHT TESTING OF THE **XPB2M-1** MARS PROTOTYPE IN JULY 1942. IT BUILT AN IMPRESSIVE SERVICE RECORD AS A TRANSPORT IN THE PACIFIC BETWEEN 1943 AND 1945 WITH ITS LONG RANGE AND HEAVY PAYLOAD. *BELOW:* THE **XPB2M-1** MARS PROTO-TYPE ON THE MARTIN RAMP AFTER REPAIRS. *OPPOSITE BOTTOM:* THE SIXTH AND FINAL MARS BUILT WAS THE **JRM-2** *CAROLINE MARS.*

LUXURY ALOFT IN THE *Martin Mars* FLYING HOTEL

1 Off to Europe, via Martin Mars. When Victory is finally won, you'll be taking that trip of your dreams . . . a two-week holiday abroad!

2 So step aboard the Mars and look about. Two full decks. Spacious, air-conditioned rooms. Courteous service. A flying hotel!

3 Note the size, smartness and comfort of the Mars' lounge! No cramped seats, or narrow aisles. Plenty of room for walking about!

4 A full-course dinner, from the Mars' galley, served by smiling stewards. Soft lights . . . gay laughter . . . music! De luxe transportation!

5 After dinner you'll want to explore the big ship. Here, for example, is the ultra-modern Skytop Room, a favorite rendezvous.

6 Your snug cabin is waiting when you're ready for bed. Nothing to disturb your slumber as the great ship speeds toward Europe and vacation.

7 Morning . . . and you're there! Only a few hours have passed. Ahead lie days of sight-seeing, adventure . . . thanks to the Martin Mars!

Fantasy? Long-range prediction? Not at all! The plane shown here is flying today! It's a Martin Mars transport! True, today's Mars contains no luxurious furnishings. Every inch of space is needed for war supplies. But commercial versions of these huge Navy transports will offer every comfort to tomorrow's trans-ocean travelers. So when you plan that trip abroad . . . plan to fly via Martin Mars!

THE GLENN L. MARTIN COMPANY, BALTIMORE 3, MD.
THE GLENN L. MARTIN-NEBRASKA CO., OMAHA

Martin AIRCRAFT

LEFT: "FANTASY?" ASKED THIS MARTIN ADVERTISEMENT FROM 1948. "LONG-RANGE PREDICTION? NOT AT ALL. THE PLANE SHOWN HERE IS FLYING TODAY!" THE PLANE WAS THE US NAVY'S JRM AND THE THRUST OF THE ADVERTISING WAS TO GENERATE A COMMERCIAL MARKET FOR THE BIG AIRCRAFT. IT PROMISED A LEVEL OF LUXURY REMINISCENT OF THE PREWAR CLIPPERS, BUT AIRLINES WERE NOW BUYING LONG-RANGE LANDPLANES AND THERE WOULD BE NO COMMERCIAL MARS, EXCEPT FOR THE WATER BOMBERS. NOR WOULD SCHEDULED AIRLINES EVER AGAIN OFFER THE AMENITIES AVAILABLE ON THE CLIPPERS AND PROMISED IN THIS ADVERTISEMENT.

BELOW: THE JRM-3 *MARIANAS MARS* DEMONSTRATING A WATER DROP IN CANADA. IN 1956, IT WAS SOLD AS A WATER BOMBER TO FLYING TANKERS LIMITED, ALONG WITH *PHILIPPINE*, *HAWAII* AND *CAROLINE MARS*. THE US NAVY HAD NAMED ITS JRMS AFTER ISLAND GROUPS IN THE PACIFIC OCEAN WHERE THEY OPERATED FOR 10 YEARS. WHEN THEY WERE SOLD, THE NEW OWNER KEPT THE GIVEN NAMES.

FACING PAGE AND BELOW RIGHT: STILL GOING AFTER HALF A CENTURY: THE JRM-3 *PHILIPPINE MARS* FLYING IN 1995 IN CANADA AS A WATER BOMBER.

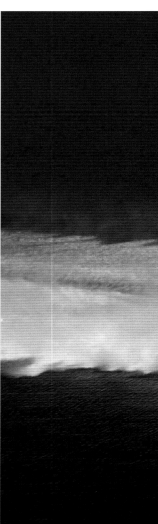

THE VOUGHT OS2U KINGFISHER

Possibly the most important single-engine American floatplane of World War II, the Kingfisher was developed in 1937 to answer a US Navy requirement for a floatplane that would be sufficiently compact to serve aboard battleships without having to fold its wings. In breaking tradition for shipboard floatplanes, Vought designer Rex Biesel proposed an all-metal monoplane that was ordered under the designation XOS2U-1.

The prototype flew on March 1, 1938, and the first operational OS2Us entered service aboard the USS *Colorado* in August 1940. The improved OS2U-2 was introduced later in the same year, and by the time the United States entered World War II, Kingfishers served not only aboard ships, but with the Navy's Inshore Patrol as well.

All the OS2Us were 30 feet 1 inch in length, 12 feet 11 inches high, and had wing spans of 35 feet 11 inches. The total wing area measured 262 square feet. The OS2U-2 weighed 3,432 pounds empty, had a gross weight of 5,229 pounds, and was powered by a Pratt & Whitney R-985-50 engine, rated at 450 horsepower at 5,000 feet. This gave the OS2U-2 a top speed of 170 mph at 5,500 feet, and a cruising speed of 116 mph. It had a service ceiling of 16,000 feet, and its range was 745 miles.

Armament consisted of a pair of .30-caliber machine guns and two 116-pound bombs. In the Inshore Patrol sub-hunting operations, Kingfishers carried a 350-pound depth charge. The first German U-boat sunk by O2SUs was the U-576, which was dispatched in July 1942 off the United States Eastern Seaboard.

During World War II, Kingfishers served wherever the the US Navy was functional, operating from destroyers as well as battleships and cruisers. Utilized mainly as scout planes, they were also used for air-sea rescue, and one Kingfisher even shot down a Japanese fighter over Iwo Jima. A total of 1,519 Kingfishers were built, most of them O2SU-3s. Of these, 100 were lend-leased to Britain, while 48 others were divided between Australia, Chile, Mexico, Uruguay and the Dominican Republic.

RIGHT: THREE **OS2U-3** KINGFISHERS IN FORMATION.
BELOW: A KINGFISHER SCOUTS A SHELL-POCKED PACIFIC
ISLAND. OPPOSITE BOTTOM: A ROYAL NAVY KINGFISHER
BEING HOISTED ABOARD THE **HMS** PEGASUS.

THE BLOHM UND VOSS BV.222 WIKING

The race to conquer the commercial air lanes across the Atlantic Ocean spawned many of the great seaplanes of the 1920s and 1930s. The theme that ran through the history of developing these aircraft was the desire to make them bigger and bigger. If a transatlantic service was to be commercially successful, it had to carry more passengers than the competition. Had it not been for World War II, the 1940s would have been the golden age of flying boat travel.

As World War II began, however, many of the intended commercial aircraft — both landplanes and seaplanes — were adapted as military aircraft, and this included the massive Blohm und Voss Bv.222 Wiking (Viking). The Bv.222 was designed by Richard Vogt for the Atlantic market and it was ordered by Deutsche Luft Hansa in 1937.

The idea was for spacious staterooms accommodating 24 passengers for day flights or 16 with sleeping arrangements. However, by the time the prototype flew on September 7, 1940, the war was under way, and the Wiking

program was taken over by the Luftwaffe. The first military operation for the Wiking prototype involved flying troops and supplies between Hamburg and Kirkenes, Norway in 1941.

The Luftwaffe was pleased with the ability of the Wiking to carry large loads over long distances, and began using it to fly supply missions to the Afrika Korps in North Africa. The presence of British interceptors in this theater demonstrated the necessity of defensive armament, and the prototype was fitted with guns that would become standard on production Bv.222s. These would be located in two upper turrets and a nose turret, as well as in fixed positions through-

RIGHT: THE PONDEROUS BV.222
WIKING IN FLIGHT. *BELOW:* A
MOORED BV.222. *OPPOSITE BOTTOM:*
BOUND FOR THE MEDITERRANEAN, A
BV.222 LIFTS OFF.

out the hull. These weapons were initially 7.9mm and 13mm machine guns, but in 1943, with the advent of the Bv.222C production model, 20mm cannons were used in the forward top turret. The gunners were aided by FuG.216R Neptun warning radar.

The first Bv.222C was the seventh Wiking. The earlier prototypes, redesignated as Bv.222A and Bv.222B, were powered by BMW/Bramo Fafnir 323R nine-cylinder radial engines rated at 1,200 horsepower for take-off with water-methanal injection. The Bv.222C was powered by six Junkers Jumo 207C 12-cylinder vertically-opposed diesel engines, each rated at 1,000 horsepower. This provided it with a top speed of 242 mph at 16,400 feet, and a cruising speed of 189 mph at sea level. It had a service ceiling of 19,700 feet, a range of 5,655 miles, and a maximum endurance of 28 hours.

The Bv.222C measured 121 feet 4.6 inches in length, 35 feet 9.2 inches high, and had a wing span of 150 feet 11 inches. The total wing area was 2,744.8 square feet. It weighed 67,572 pounds empty, and had a gross weight of 108,030 pounds. By using rocket-assisted take-off, the gross weight could be increased to 114,640.

The Wiking was used to carry both freight and troops. As a troop-carrier, it could accommodate 92 fully-equipped soldiers, and in medical evacuation configuration, it could carry 72 stretchers. By the end of 1942, the Bv.222 fleet had carried 17,778 troops and 1,453 tons of supplies to North Africa, and had evacuated 2,491 casualties. In 1942, meanwhile, two of the Bv.222s were sent to France for patrol operations over the Bay of Biscay, which were often coordinated with U-boat activities. Usually the Wikings were easy prey for Allied fighters, but in one instance of air-to-air combat, a Bv.222 shot down a Lancaster bomber.

The Wikings continued in service and in production until 1944, when the deterioration of German industrial capacity forced a refocusing on building fighters and spare parts for fighters. Three Wikings survived the war, but were scrapped —

two of them in the United States — after having been evaluated by the Allies.

Two examples of the Bv.238, which was a larger, 176,370-gross weight flying boat based on the Bv.222, were built, but that program was also terminated in 1944. The Bv.238 was 142 feet 8.5 inches in length, 42 feet 11 inches high, and had a wing span of 197 feet 4.75 inches. The total wing area was 3,928.83 square feet. The Bv.238 was powered by six Daimler-Benz DB.603V 12-cylinder, liquid-cooled radial engines, each rated at 1,750 horsepower. This gave it a top speed of 264 mph at 19,685 feet, and a cruising speed of 253 mph at the same altitude. It would have had a maximum range of 8,700 miles in its patrol bomber configuration.

While the Martin Mars was larger than the Blohm und Voss boats, and it *would* go into production after the war, only one aircraft was operational during the war. This gave the Wiking the distinction of being the largest seaplane to be in production during World War II.

RIGHT: **A WIKING OVER THE NORTH ATLANTIC.** *BELOW:* **AN EARLY BV.222 AT REST, CIRCA 1942. NOTE THE RADIAL ENGINES AND THE GUN TURRETS.**

THE MARTIN PBM MARINER

The Martin Mariner patrol bomber was probably the earliest American boat to both serve in World War II and also have a long and meaningful postwar career with the US Navy. The Glenn L. Martin Company began work on the project in 1937, and the prototype XPBM-1 first flew on February 18, 1939. Between November 1940 and April 1941, the US Navy ordered 559 production Mariners under the designation PBM-3. The designations PBM-2 and PBM-4 were assigned to variants not built, and there were 20 PBM-1s delivered in 1940. While the prototype and PBM-1 had retractable floats, the PBM-3 production planes would have fixed floats to save weight.

The PBM-3 was 79 feet 9.9 inches in length, 21 feet 6.2 inches high, and had a wing span of 118 feet. The total wing area measured 1,408 square feet. It weighed 33,175 pounds empty, and had a gross weight of 58,000 pounds. Mariners were powered by various Wright Cyclone 14-cylinder radial engines, such as the R-2600-22, each rated at 1,900 horsepower. This gave the aircraft a top speed of 211 mph at 16,000 feet, and a cruising speed of 127 mph at 1,500 feet. It had a service ceiling of 19,800 feet, and its range was 2,240 miles.

The first PBM-3 was the PBM-3R 20-passenger transport variant, of which 50 were delivered to the Naval Air Transport Service. The first patrol-bomber versions were the PBM-3C,

RIGHT: AUGUST 1943 - ROYAL AIR FORCE MARINER GR.1s IN AUGUST 1943. IN THE BACKGROUND IS THE XPB2M-1R MARS PROTOTYPE. *BELOW:* PBM-1s UNDER CONSTRUCTION AT MARTIN'S MIDDLE RIVER PLANT IN MAY 1940. *OPPOSITE BOTTOM:* A PBM-5 ON SAIPAN IN 1945. IN THE FOREGROUND IS THE TAIL OF A NIGHTMARE MARINER NIGHT BOMBER. IN THE BACKGROUND ARE A CONSOLIDATED **PBY** AND A **PB2Y**.

of which 272 were delivered after September 1942, and the similar PBM-3D, of which 201 were built. These were equipped with powered gun turrets in the bow and atop the fuselage, each of which carried .50-caliber machine guns. The PBM-3D also had a powered tail turret with a pair of machine guns.

The PBM-3B was the US Navy designation for 32 aircraft delivered to Britain in 1943, under the British Designation Mariner GR.I. The same as the PBM-3C, the Mariner GR.Is were operated by a Royal Air Force Coastal Command squadron off the western coast of Scotland.

The first of 156 PBM-3S anti-submarine Mariners was delivered in July 1943, equipped with search radar and with no forward turrets. A dozen of the PBM-3S Mariners would be delivered to Australia. In service with the US Navy, Mariners were operational in both the Atlantic and the Pacific, and PBM-3Ss operated from bases in the United States on submarine-hunting patrols.

The final production Mariner would be the PBM-5, which succeeded the PBM-3D on the assembly line in June 1944. The PBM-5 was powered by the Pratt & Whitney R-2800-34 Wasp engine rated at 2,100 horsepower at take-off. The PBM-5 remained in production until the end of 1945. A total of 592 were produced. They would remain in service with the US Navy, operating both from shore and from seaplane tenders, well into the 1950s.

The offensive armament carried by the early Mariners was stored in bomb bays located in the engine nacelles aft of the engines. Eight 500 to 1,600-pound bombs could be accommodated, and Mariners typically carried a variety of bombs along with 325-pound depth bombs or four Mk.13 mines. A pair of Mk.13 torpedoes could also be transported outside the bomb bay. The PBM-3S typically carried eight depth bombs.

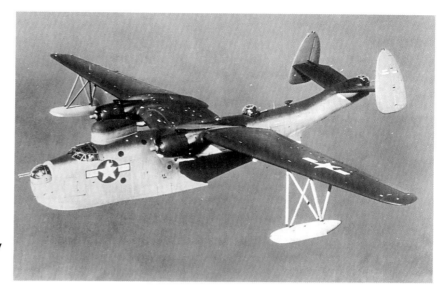

RIGHT: **A MARTIN PBM-5**, THE ULTIMATE *MARINER*. *BELOW AND OPPOSITE BOTTOM:* CREWS SECURE A **PBM-1** WITH A BOW LINE AT NAVAL AIR STATION BANANA RIVER IN FLORIDA, THEN HAUL IT ASHORE TO BE HOSED DOWN.

THE MARTIN P5M MARLIN

The development of seaplanes by the US Navy diminished dramatically after World War II. Long-range landplanes now had the capability to take on the patrol functions of the great flying boats, and helicopters would soon replace the catapult-launched floatplanes. The only seaplane to be acquired in significant numbers after the war would be the Martin Marlin.

A successor to the PBM Mariner, the XP5M-1 was based on new technology in hull design. Ordered by the Navy in June 1946, the Marlin had a PBM wing, but a long, narrow hull that made it cleaner hydrodynamically than its predecessor.

The prototype first flew on May 30, 1948, and production models joined the fleet in December 1951. They carried a huge APS-44A radar radome in the nose in place of a gun turret, and were armed with homing torpedoes and depth charges in bomb bays aft of the engines. The 160 P5M-1s were followed by 117 P5M-2s. The latter remained in production until December 1960, making them the last large flying boats to be built in the United States.

The P5M-2 measured 100 feet 2 inches in length, 30 feet 11 inches high, and had a wing span of 118 feet 2 inches. The total wing area was 1,406 square feet. It weighed 49,218 pounds empty, and had a gross weight of 76,595 pounds. It was powered by a pair of Wright R-3350-32WA radial engines, each rated at 3,700 horsepower at take-off. This provided the Marlin with a top speed of 266 mph at 17,400 feet, and a cruising speed of 159 mph. It had a service ceiling of 20,600 feet, its ferry range was 3,060 miles, and its range when loaded for combat was 2,471 miles.

Redesignated as SP-5 in 1962, many Marlins were retrofitted with APS-80 search radar, ASQ-8 magnetic anomaly detectors, and provisions for two Mk.43 torpedoes or four 2,025-pound Mk.39 mines. The 20mm cannons were deleted from the tail turrets, but when Marlins flew patrol missions along the Vietnam coast in 1965, M60 machine guns were carried and fired from side hatches.

The Marlin was present at the end of an era. The last US Navy squadron to operate seaplanes — VP-40 at Naval Air Station North Island in San Diego Bay — retired its last SP-5 Marlins on November 6, 1967, thus ending a 56-year Navy seaplane tradition that had begun with Glenn Curtiss at the same place in 1911.

RIGHT: A P5M-2S MARLIN WITH MAGNETIC ANOMALY
DETECTION (MAD) EQUIPMENT INSTALLED IN A FAIRING
MOUNTED HIGH ON THE TAIL. DIRECTION-FINDING EQUIP-
MENT DOGHOUSE IS VISIBLE AFT OF THE COCKPIT.
BELOW: TWO P5M-2 MARLINS (MODEL 237B) MOORED.
OPPOSITE BOTTOM: A P5M-1 MARLIN BECOMES AIRBORNE
WITH JET-ASSISTED TAKEOFF (JATO) CANISTERS ON THE
AFT FUSELAGE.

THE MARTIN P6M SEAMASTER

The SeaMaster was an aircraft both ahead of its time and behind its time. As a jet flying boat, it was a great leap forward in technology for the early 1950s; however, as a US Navy flying boat, it arrived at least a decade after the era when flying boats were an integral and essential element of naval aviation.

SeaMaster design development began in 1952 in response to a Navy request for a fast, combat-capable reconnaissance and mine-laying seaplane. The speed requirements dictated that it should be a jet. Martin won the contract over the competing Convair design, and the XP6M-1 made its first flight on July 14, 1955. The test flight demonstrated better hydrodynamic performance than expected.

In what might have been considered an omen, both XP6M-1 aircraft were lost during test flights, but the production prototype YP6M-1 made its first flight in January 1958. Measuring 134 feet 4 inches in length, 33 feet 9 inches high, it had a wing span of 102 feet 7 inches. The total

wing area was 1,900 square feet. It weighed 84,685 pounds empty, and had a gross weight of 167,011 pounds. The YP6M-1 was powered by four Allison J71-A-6 turbojet engines, each delivering 9,500 pounds of thrust. This gave the aircraft a top speed of 646 mph at 5,000 feet. It had a service ceiling of 35,000 feet, its patrol range was 2,745 miles, and it had a range was 1,595 miles when mines.

The armament consisted of two 20mm cannons in the tail turret, and provisions for 30,000 pounds of mines or other payloads. The ordnance was carried internally in a bomb bay with watertight seals around the rotating doors. The SeaMaster used a rotary bomb delivery system that Martin had developed for the XB-51 Air Force bomber, in which the ordnance was attached to the inside of the door and rotated out rather than being dropped. Cameras on the reconnaissance version would also be mounted here.

RIGHT: ALL SIX SERVICE-TEST **YP6M-1**S LINED UP ON THEIR BEACHING GEAR IN FRONT OF THE STRAWBERRY POINT HANGAR IN 1958. *BELOW:* A **P6M-2** SEAMASTER IN FLIGHT. WITH MORE POWERFUL ENGINES AND HEAVIER GROSS WEIGHT THAN THE PROTOTYPE OR SERVICE-TEST AIRCRAFT, THE PRODUCTION SEAMASTERS SAT LOWER IN THE WATER. *OPPOSITE BOTTOM:* THE SECOND **XP6M-1** SEAMASTER PROTOTYPE, WITH WHITE UNDERSURFACES, IS ROLLED OUT OF THE MARTIN PLANT IN NOVEMBER 1955. THE FIRST PROTOTYPE HAD ROLLED OUT IN SECRECY 11 MONTHS EARLIER.

Unlike previous flying boats, the SeaMaster was designed to "live" in the water and not to require beaching for long periods.

A total of six YP6M-1s were produced, and the US Navy ordered 24 P6M-2 production aircraft. The P6M-2 was 134 feet in length, 31 feet high, and had a wing span of 100 feet. The total wing area measured 1,900 square feet. It weighed 84,000 pounds empty, and had a gross weight of 160,000 pounds.

The P6M-2 was powered by four Allison J75-P-2 turbojet engines, each delivering 15,800 pounds of thrust, giving the aircraft a top speed of 686 mph at sea level. It had a service ceiling of 43,900 feet, and its range was 868 miles with a full payload of 30,000 pounds of mines.

The P6M-2 made its first flight on March 3, 1959, and three aircraft were completed by August, when the Navy abruptly cancelled the program. The SeaMasters then in service, as well as all the ancillary basing and maintenance equipment, were scrapped.

The reason for the termination seems to have been based purely on budgetary concerns. Of the $470 million that had been allocated, $400 million had already been spent. Critics argued that cancellation would mean savings of $70 million, but proponents cited the investment already made and the value of the 10 aircraft in service. The critics won.

The P6M program marked the end of two eras. It was the last new flying boat acquired by the US Navy (although the P5M would continue in service after the P6M), and it was the last aircraft ever built by Martin. The company turned to the production of missiles, particularly the Titan II ICBM and the Titan III family of space launch vehicles.

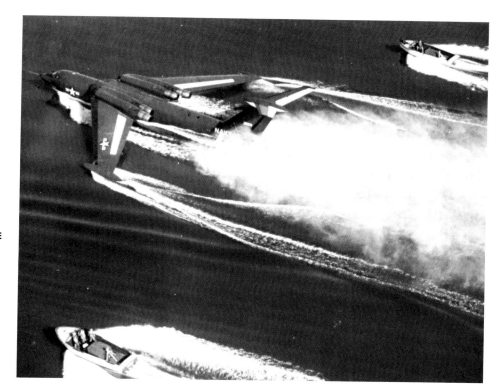

RIGHT: THE FIRST **YP6M-1** SEAMASTER PROTOTYPE IS FLANKED BY TWO ESCORT BOATS AS IT TAXIES ON MIDDLE RIVER, MARYLAND. *BELOW:* A **P6M-2** SEAMASTER DURING A HIGH-SPEED TAXI. WITH 63,200 POUNDS OF THRUST, THE **P6M-2** REACHED AN UNOFFICIAL SPEED OF MACH 1.02 DURING A FLIGHT TEST. PILOTS REPORTED THAT IT HANDLED WELL AND WAS CAPABLE OF FLYING AT MACH .89 "ON THE DECK." *OPPOSITE BOTTOM:* THE FIRST **XP6M-1** PROTOTYPE DURING ITS FIRST FLIGHT.

THE CONVAIR P5Y/R3Y TRADEWIND

Although the US Navy would make a shift from flying boats to landplanes as patrol bombers in the late 1940s, the importance of the wartime flying boats still guided acquisition policy in the years immediately after World War II. In 1946, there was still a persistent belief in the continued development of seaplanes, especially as advances in technology had resulted in longer, narrower and more hydrodynamically efficient hulls that promised better performance. Two clear examples of this were the Martin P6M Marlin and the Convair P5Y. The latter also incorporated the Navy's interest in using the new turboprop engines on a large flying boat.

Convair was an energetic San Diego-based firm with a strong flying boat heritage that included the Consolidated PBY Catalina and PB2Y Coronado. ("Convair" was the commonly-used contraction for Consolidated Vultee Aircraft Corporation, which was the result of the 1941 merger of Consolidated and Vultee, but it would not be an officially registered trademark until 1954.)

The P5Y was conceived during the war by Convair's Hydrodynamic Research Laboratory, and developed under the guidance of laboratory director Ernest Stout. The XP5Y prototype took shape slowly, due to problems with the extremely complex engines. The XP5Y-1 was powered by four Allison XT40-A-4 turboprop engines, each rated at 5,100 shaft horse power, driving eight huge contra-rotating propellers. The XT40 was actually a pair of T38s linked to the props through a complicated reduction gear mechanism.

The XP5Y finally made its first flight on April 18, 1950, with test pilot Sam Shannon at the controls. Measuring 127 feet 11 inches in length, 46 feet 2 inches high, the XP5Y-1 had a wing span of 145 feet 9.9 inches. The total wing area consisted of 2,102 square feet. It weighed 71,824

RIGHT: **THE SIXTH AND LAST R3Y-2 TRANSPORTS OVER SAN DIEGO.** *BELOW:* **A LONG-NOSED R3Y-1 COMES IN FOR A LANDING IN HEAVY SEAS.** *OPPOSITE BOTTOM:* **THE XP5Y-1 IN FLIGHT. NOTE THE SIDE-BLISTER TURRETS THAT WOULD HAVE HELD GUNS IN A PRODUCTION MODEL.**

pounds empty, and had a gross weight of 140,374 pounds. The aircraft achieved a top speed of 388 mph at 5,000 feet, and a cruising speed of 225 mph. It had a service ceiling of 39,700 feet, and its range was 3,450 miles without payload, or 2,785 miles with eight 325-pound depth charges.

Flight testing of the first prototype continued for three years, with no production order until the aircraft crashed during a dive test off Point Loma, near San Diego, in July 1953. The second prototype was scrapped without having made its first flight.

In the meantime, the US Navy had contracted with Convair to build a transport variant of the XP5Y to augment and eventually replace its fleet of Martin Mars transports. Designated as R3Y and known as the Tradewind, the transport version first flew on February 25, 1954, and a year later it broke a transcontinental seaplane speed record of 403 mph — a record that still stands today.

The R3Y-2 was 139 feet 88.4 inches in length, 51 feet 5 inches high, and had a wing span of 145 feet 9.9 inches. The total wing area measured 2,102 square feet. It had a normal gross weight of 145,500 pounds, or a maximum gross weight of 165,000 pounds. The R3Y-2 was powered by four Allison T40-A-10 turboprop engines.

In 1956, the Navy began to put its five R3Y-1s and six R3Y-2s into service on its vast transpacific supply routes. While the Mars transports were named for islands in the Pacific, the Tradewinds were named for bodies of water adjacent to the Pacific.

In 1956, four Tradewinds were converted to serve as aerial tankers, and an R3Y was the first aircraft to simultaneously refuel four others. However, severe turbulence problems arose due to the outboard refueling hoses being longer than the others and the project was cancelled.

Use of the R3Y as an assault transport — a sort of flying landing craft — was considered, as was its use as a test-bed in the nuclear-powered aircraft program, but both of these ideas were not pursued.

In the end, it was the problems caused by the complexity of its engines, rather than its other qualities, that caused the demise of the R3Y. In 1957 and 1958, serious, albeit non-fatal, engine mishaps with the *Indian Ocean Tradewind* and the *Coral Sea Tradewind* caused the Navy to withdraw and scrap the Tradewind fleet. It was a sad end to an aircraft that would have had great potential with proper engines.

RIGHT: THIS **R3Y-2** TRADEWIND IS CON-
FIGURED FOR IN-FLIGHT REFUELLING.
BELOW: THE TRADEWIND, SEEN HERE
WITH A BRACE OF GRUMMAN **F9F**
COUGARS, WAS THE FIRST AIRCRAFT TO
REFUEL FOUR OTHERS SIMULTANEOUSLY.
OPPOSITE BOTTOM: THE MARINES HAVE
LANDED! WITH ITS HUGE TILT-UP NOSE,
THE **R3Y-2** WAS PROPOSED AS A FLYING
LANDING CRAFT. HOWEVER, IT WOULD
HAVE BEEN VERY VULNERABLE TO
GROUND FIRE IN THIS MODE.

THE HUGHES HK-1 "SPRUCE GOOSE"

No survey of seaplanes would be complete without a look at the biggest of them all, the airplane officially called the HK-1 Hercules, but much more widely known as the "Spruce Goose." It was the brain child of the eccentric industrialist, Howard Robard Hughes. Hughes was an amazing character — a reclusive billionaire, whose obsessive-compulsive disorder and bizarre behavior cut him off from the world for the last decade of his life. Before that, however, he had been a brilliant inventor, an Academy Award-winning movie producer, and a dare-devil pilot who set an around-the-world speed record in 1938.

During World War II, as German U-boats were taking a severe toll on Allied shipping, Hughes and shipbuilder Henry J. Kaiser came up with the idea to build giant airplanes to fly over the U-boats. Hughes and Kaiser received United States government funding for the project on the condition that they would not make a profit, and Hughes began construction in Culver City, California.

Hughes conceived the idea of building the big aircraft out of wood. It was widely believed that this was impossible, but Hughes used the Duramold process, which he had invented, to glue and laminate the layers of wood. Contrary to its nickname, the HK-1 was built primarily of birch, not spruce. It was 219 feet in length, 79 feet 3 inches high, and had a wing span of 320 feet. Its gross weight was 400,000 pounds, more than double that of the Martin Mars, which was the largest airplane in the world when the Spruce Goose was conceived. The big boat was powered by eight Pratt & Whitney R-4360 Wasp Major 28-cylinder, air-cooled radial engines, each rated at 3,000 horsepower. This gave the Spruce Goose a theoretical cruising speed of 175 mph. Its range — also theoretical because it was never tested — was 3,500 miles. It would have carried 500 to 700 people.

The war ended before the HK-1 was finished and Hughes faced not only ridicule, but a Congressional investigation for his apparent boondoggle. In response to his critics, Hughes made a one-mile flight in the HK-1 on November 2, 1947. It was billed as the plane's first taxi test, but Hughes, who was at the controls himself, knew that it would be the first and only flight. Afterward, Hughes stored the aircraft in a climate-controlled hangar, where it was maintained in flyable condition until 1980, four years after Hughes' death.

In 1982, amid a great deal of fanfare, the Spruce Goose was placed on display in what was the world's largest geodesic dome overlooking Long Beach Harbor. In 1992, it was sold to the Evergreen Adventure Museum in McMinneville, Oregon. The Spruce Goose was disassembled and barged to Oregon, where it has remained, awaiting an uncertain future.

RIGHT: THESE MASSIVE HAMILTON STANDARD PROPS TURNED FOR ONLY ONE FLIGHT. *BELOW*: FINAL ASSEMBLY AT TERMINAL ISLAND IN LONG BEACH HARBOR, CIRCA 1946. *OPPOSITE BOTTOM*: THE HK-1 ON THE MOVE IN OCTOBER 1980.

THE CONVAIR SEADART

During World War I, the Italy-based Macchi had broken new ground with the development of its M.5 seaplane fighter. However, it was an idea that would remain largely dormant for many years. There were experiments with putting fighters on floats, and observation floatplanes occasionally flew interceptor missions, but fighters were generally conceived, built, and operated as landplanes.

After World War II, however, two seaplane jet fighters were prototyped, the Saunders-Roe SR.A/1 in Britain (the world's first turbojet seaplane), and the Convair SeaDart.

In the case of the SeaDart, the program would include an innovation for which Convair was the pioneer: delta wings. Convair engineers looked into using a 45-degree sweep, but decided they could do better. The result was a 60-degree sweep which provided an ingenious triangular, or delta-shaped, wing that eliminated the need for horizontal tail surfaces. The world's first true delta-winged aircraft, Convair's XF-92 research aircraft, made its maiden flight in 1948, and this design was incorporated into the F-102 interceptor which flew in 1953.

Meanwhile, the US Navy requested Convair to build what was destined to be the world's first seaplane that would also double as a high-performance delta-winged jet fighter. The design for this amazing craft was based on an amalgam of Convair's blended-hull fuselage design and a wing design similar to that envisioned for the F-102. The

Navy ordered a dozen aircraft under the designation F2Y-1, and the prototype XF2Y-1 made its first flight on April 9, 1953. It was 52 feet 7 inches in length, 16 feet 2 inches high with its skis retracted, 20 feet 9 inches with its skis extended, and had a wing span of 33 feet 8 inches. The total wing area measured 568 square feet. It weighed 12,625 pounds empty, and had a gross weight of 16,527 pounds.

The XF2Y-1 was powered by two Westinghouse J46-WE-12B turbojet engines, each delivering 5,725 pounds of thrust. This gave the SeaDart a top speed of 994 mph at 35,000 feet, a service ceiling of 54,800 feet, and its range was 513 miles.

The XF2Y-1, equipped with a pair of skis for its water take-offs, was joined by a second service test YF2Y-1 with a single ski. It was in this aircraft that Convair test pilot Chuck Richbourg became the first — and only — man to break the sound barrier in a seaplane on August 3, 1954. Sadly, Richbourg was to lose his life only three months later, when the YF2Y-1 exploded during a low level pass over San Diego Bay.

A third SeaDart joined the test program in 1955 and flight testing continued through 1957. Though five aircraft completed over 500 test flights, the SeaDart never went into production because of persistent vibration problems, and possibly because of the overall eccentricity of the seaplane jet fighter concept.

RIGHT: THE YF2Y-1 SEADART OVER SAN DIEGO, WHERE IT WAS DESIGNED AND BUILT. BELOW: THE YF2Y-1 SEADART DURING TAXI TESTS IN 1954. OPPOSITE BOTTOM: THE XF2Y-1 GATHERING SPEED FOR TAKE-OFF.

THE GRUMMAN GOOSE

The first Grumman aircraft developed for the non-military market, the Model G-21 Goose made its first flight in May 1937, and over 200 were sold within 15 months. A durable, easy-to-maintain amphibian, it seated eight, and found a ready market in the late 1930s among private individuals and companies in North America, Australia, Britain, Venezuela, and the Netherlands East Indies.

The Royal Canadian Air Force became the first military customer in 1938. The US Navy and US Army Air Corps also ordered Geese as utility transports and observation amphibians under the J3F and OA-9 designations. The Portuguese navy acquired a Goose in 1939, and air services of several Latin American nations brought them into their inventories during World War II. After World War II, they served with French forces in Indochina and later in West Africa, operating from rivers and lakes, and from off-shore seaplane tenders.

The Goose measured 38 feet 3 inches in length and had a wing span of 49 feet. It had a gross weight of 7,500 pounds. The Goose was originally powered by a pair of Pratt & Whitney R-985-AN-6 radial engines, each rated at

450 horsepower. This gave the Goose a top speed of 195 mph at sea level. It had a range of 1,150 miles. In the 1950s, many aircraft would be retrofitted with Pratt & Whitney of Canada PT6A turboprop engines rated at 680 shaft horsepower.

The G-21G Turbo-Goose, as it was called, was also enlarged and retrofitted with upgraded equipment. It was was 39 feet 7 inches in length and had a wing span of 50 feet 10 inches. It had a gross weight of 12,500 pounds. The Turbo-Goose had a service ceiling of 20,000 feet and a range of 1,600 miles. Most of the upgrades and retrofits were undertaken by McKinnon Enterprises of Sandy, Oregon, and by its successor, McKinnon-Viking of Sidney, British Columbia.

Grumman concluded Goose production in 1945, but the aircraft entered a new life as surplus JRFs and OA-9s entered the market. This attracted the interest of small airlines from British Columbia to the Caribbean. Still in service at the end of the century, the Goose has proven itself to be an ideal aircraft for low-density routes that connect many small island communities.

RIGHT: **A CATALINA AIR LINES GOOSE WELCOMES PASSENGERS AS ANOTHER WAITS OFF-SHORE.** *BELOW:* **JRF-2 GEESE AWAIT DELIVERY AT THE GRUMMAN PLANT DURING WORLD WAR II.** *OPPOSITE BOTTOM:* **A PRIVATE-LY-OWNED GOOSE TAXIS OUT FOR AN INTER-ISLAND HOP.**

THE GRUMMAN WIDGEON

The G-44 was conceived by Grumman in 1939 as a low-cost alternative to the popular Grumman Goose. Essentially, it was a scaled-down Goose, a small amphibious aircraft for the general aviation market. In keeping with the convention adopted earlier with the Grumman Duck and the Goose, it was named for an aquatic bird.

The prototype XG-44 Widgeon made its debut flight from Bethpage, Long Island on June 28, 1940, with Bud Gilles and Roy Grumman himself at the dual controls. Orders for 51 aircraft had been received by the time that deliveries began in 1941.

The G-44 Widgeon was 31 feet 1 inch in length, 11 feet 5 inches high, and had a wing span of 40 feet. The total wing area comprised 245 square feet. It weighed 3,240 pounds empty, and had a gross weight of 4,525 pounds.

The G-44 was powered by a variety of engine types, originally a pair of Ranger 6-440C-5 six-cylinder air-cooled radial engine driving two-bladed props and each rated at 200 horsepower. This gave the Widgeon a top speed of 153 mph at sea level, and a cruising speed of 138 mph. It had a service ceiling of 14,600 feet, while its range was 920 miles.

When the United States entered World War II in December 1941, Goose production shifted from the lucrative commercial market to the military. The US Coast Guard was to buy 25 Widgeons under the designation J4F-1, and the US Navy acquired 131 as J4F-2s, one of which would be credited with a U-boat kill off the coast of Louisiana.

Of the J4F-2s, 14 were transferred to Brazil under the designation UC4F-2, and 15 were delivered to Britain's Royal Navy. For distinguishing purposes, the Royal Navy initially designated their aircraft as the Gosling Mk.I, although the name Widgeon Mk.I was adopted in 1944. Most of the British aircraft were assigned to duty in the Caribbean. The US Army Air Forces commandeered 15 commercial G-44s at the beginning of the war under the observation amphibian designation OA-14.

Other sales of Widgeons included three to Pan American Airways, not as airliners but as seaplane training aircraft. Portugal's navy, earlier a customer for the Grumman Goose, acquired a dozen Widgeons in 1941, and the air force of Thailand bought a pair.

Grumman ceased production of the Widgeon in 1949 after producing 276 aircraft. In 1948, however, Grumman licensed Société de Constructions Aéro-navales (SCAN) in France to build Widgeons in that country. The SCAN Widgeons were powered by Mathis 8G40 eight-cylinder 190-horsepower engines. Sales of French-built Widgeons got off to a slow start when the first one crashed into the Seine in 1949, seriously injuring the famous aviator Jacqueline Auriol. Sales were modest in France, but hoped-for sales to the French government were disappointing. Only 41 aircraft were built and three were bought by the government. One notable aircraft was sold to Emperor Bao Dai of Vietnam.

In the 1950s, McKinnon Enterprises of Sandy, Oregon began a re-engining program to create a "Super Widgeon." The McKinnon Super Widgeon had the same dimensions as the G-44, but was powered by Lycoming flat-six engines, either the 260-horsepower GO-435-C2B or the 270-horsepower GO-480-B1D. This gave the Super Widgeon a top speed of 190 mph at sea level, and a cruising speed of 175 mph. It had a service ceiling of 18,000 feet, while its range was 1,000 miles.

RIGHT AND BELOW: **THE EXTREMELY DURABLE GRUMMAN G-44 WIDGEONS REMAINED IN SERVICE WITH PRIVATE INDIVIDUALS AND SMALL AIR SERVICES UNTIL THE** 1980s.

THE GRUMMAN MALLARD

The Mallard was created by Grumman late in World War II in anticipation of a significant postwar market for a 10 to 15-passenger amphibian capable of being used by feeder airlines. The initial thrust in the design process had been to simply create an improved G-21 Goose, but initial customer response was lukewarm so Grumman went back to the drawing board.

The G-73 Mallard was larger than the Goose and had a tricycle landing gear for land operations. It was 48 feet 4 inches in length, 18 feet 9 inches high, and had a wing span of 66 feet 8 inches. The total wing area measured 444 square feet. It weighed 9,350 pounds empty, and had a gross weight of 12,750 pounds.

The Mallard was powered by a pair of Pratt & Whitney Wasp S3H1 nine-cylinder radial engines, each rated at 600 horsepower. This gave the Mallard a top speed of 215 mph at 6,000 feet, and a cruising speed of 180 mph. It had a service ceiling of 23,000 feet, and a range of 1,380 miles with an 810-pound payload.

The Mallard first flew on April 30, 1946, while commercial deliveries began in September. By March 1951, a total of 56 would be sold to customers in the United States, Canada and the United Kingdom. A pair of Mallards with plush interiors were sold to the government of Egypt for the use of King Farouk, and these continued in service after his majesty was overthrown in 1952.

The termination of Mallard production was a result of both mediocre sales and the lack of aluminum, which was deemed a critical material during the Korean War and was hence scarce.

Despite the poor Mallard sales experienced by Grumman, the second hand market was substantial, and many of the Mallards remained in service for several decades.

In 1964 and 1968, two separate projects were undertaken to retrofit Mallards with turboprop engines. The 1968 conversion resulted in the TurboMallard, which was marketed with 652-horsepower PT6A-27 engines. As late as the 1980s, five Turbo-Mallards were still in service with the Miami-based Chalks International Airline.

RIGHT: **A WASP-POWERED MALLARD IN CALIFORNIA, CIRCA 1976.** *BELOW:* **THE MALLARD KNOWN AS CAT CAYER IN MIAMI, CIRCA 1968.** *OPPOSITE BOTTOM:* **AN AUSTRALIAN TURBOMALLARD, CIRCA 1984.**

RECENT DORNIER SEAPLANES

During the 1980s, two important efforts were made to revive the great Dornier seaplanes of the past. The Dornier Seastar was the brain child of Claudius Dornier, the eldest son of the aviation pioneer, who had worked with his father until the elder Dornier's death in 1969, and who had served as chairman of Dornier GmbH until 1981.

The Seastar was an effort to recreate the old Dornier Wal using turboprop engines. Measuring 36 feet 5 inches in length, 14 feet 5.25 inches high, it had a wing span of 50 feet 10.25 inches. The total wing area was 306.6 square feet. It weighed 5,291 pounds empty, and had a gross weight of 9,259 pounds. The Seastar was powered by a pair of Pratt & Whitney Canada PT6A-11 turboprop engines mounted in tandem in a single nacelle, each rated at 500 shaft horse-power. This gave the Seastar a cruising speed of 208 mph at 9,840 feet. It had a maximum range of 1,162 miles, and a range of 621 miles with nine passengers. Passenger capacity was, however, set at 12. Dornier made extensive use of light-weight carbon fiber composites in the construction of the aircraft.

To build the Seastar, Dornier founded a company called Claudius Dornier Seastar GmbH, which was separate from Dornier GmbH, which was jointly owned by the Dornier family and Daimler-Benz GmbH. The debut flight of the first of two Seastar prototypes came on August 17, 1984, and it was announced that deliveries of production aircraft would begin in 1987.

By 1989, the production prototype, designated CD.2, was flying, but deliveries were postponed until 1990. This plan never came to fruition, however, and Dornier Seastar began a joint venture with Flitestar Angkasa, a Malaysian company. The plan of the partnership was to start manufacturing the aircraft in Penang in 1994. The project was supported by the Malaysian government, who saw it as an opportunity to make Penang a center for aircraft manufacturing; but in 1996, it was announced that the plans had been abandoned due to internal problems faced by the Malaysian firm.

Another revival project originated with Dornier GmbH itself and called for bringing back the Do.24, the trimotor flying boat from the 1940s that was produced in larger numbers than any German flying boat in history. This project also called for turboprop engines and the extensive use of carbon composite structural material. Based on a vintage Do.24 hull, the Do.24TT (Technology Testbed) first flew in April 1983. Like the Seastar, the project achieved successful flight testing for the prototype, but not the hoped-for commercial success.

The Do.24TT measured 71 feet 11 inches in length, 21 feet 11 inches high, and had a wing span of 98 feet 6 inches. It weighed 22,450 pounds empty, and had a gross weight of 34,100 pounds. The Do.24TT was powered by three Pratt & Whitney Canada PT6A-45 turboprop engines mounted on the top wing as with the original Do.24. This gave the Do.24TT a top speed of 230 mph.

RIGHT: **THE FIRST CLAUDIUS DORNIER SEASTAR MADE ITS DEBUT IN 1984 IN HAMBURG. THE SECOND SEASTAR HAD OVAL WINDOWS.** *BELOW:* **THE DO.24TT, SEEN HERE IN 1983, BROUGHT BACK MEMORIES OF THE ELEGANT DO.24 OF THE 1940S. THIS PROJECT DID NOT MOVE BEYOND THE EXPERIMENTAL STAGE.**

THE deHAVILLAND BEAVER

There is hardly a lake, bay or inlet anywhere in North America where the Beaver is a stranger. It was born before the mid-point of the twentieth century, and it will be a common sight well into the twenty-first.

The DHC-2 Beaver was developed by de Havilland Aircraft of Canada to provide communications into regions of Canada where there are few or seasonal roads. The Beaver made its first flight on August 16, 1947.

The extremely durable Beaver was a commercial success, and ultimately almost 1,700 were sold. Of these, 968 were acquired by the US Air Force under the liaison designation L-20, which was later changed to the utility designation U-6. The British government also purchased the Beaver, as did the air arms of 15 other nations.

The Beaver, including surplus military aircraft, has remained popular with the bush pilots of Alaska and Cana-da for half a century. It is 30 feet 4 inches in length, 9 feet high, and has a wing span of 48 feet. It has a gross take-off weight of 5,100 pounds. The Beaver DHC-2 Mk.I is powered by a Pratt & Whitney R-985-AN-6B or AN-14B Wasp Junior nine-cylinder radial engine, rated at 450 horsepower. This gives the Beaver Mk.I a cruising speed of 130 mph. Its service ceiling is 18,000 feet, and its range is 460 miles.

In December 1963, de Havilland introduced the Mk.III Turbo Beaver conversion, which is powered by a Pratt & Whitney Canada PT6D-6 or PT6A-20 turboprop engine rated at 550 shaft horsepower. Of the 60 Turbo Beavers, 28 went to the Ontario Department of Lands & Forests, two ski-equipped Mk.IIIs were part of a joint British-Australian Antarctic expedition, and the balance were sold to private parties in the United States and Cana-da. Many are still operational.

RIGHT: A CENTRAL BRITISH COLUMBIA BEAVER READY TO ACCEPT PASSENGERS. *BELOW:* AUTUMN COMES EARLY IN ALASKA, BUT THE BEAVER IS UNDAUNTED. *OPPOSITE BOTTOM:* A THUNDERBIRD AIR BEAVER ON A LAKE-TO-LAKE HOP.

THE GRUMMAN ALBATROSS

The Grumman G-64 project was initiated by the US Navy during World War II as a replacement for the smaller Grumman JRF Goose. Designated XJR2F-1 and originally known as the Pelican, the G-64 made its first flight on October 1, 1947. Ironically, by this time, the US Navy had largely lost interest in seaplanes, but the US Air Force — newly formed from the wartime USAAF — was very interested.

Under the National Security Act which created an independent US Air Force, that agency was given the task of conducting air-sea rescue operations for all services, and the G-64 had all the right stuff for such a job. The Navy acquired 110 G-64s under the utility designation UF-1, while the US Coast Guard received 83 and the Air Force bought nearly 300 under the search amphibian designation SA-16A.

The SA-16A Albatross measured 60 feet 8 inches in length, 24 feet 3 inches high, and had a wing span of 80 feet. The total wing area was 833 square feet. It weighed 20,815 pounds empty, and had a gross weight of 33,000 pounds. It was designed with accommodations for 12 stretchers and a crew of four to six. It was also equipped with AN/APS-31A search radar, which accounted for the distinctive radome in the Albatross' nose.

The SA-16A was powered by a pair of Wright R-1820-76A nine-cylinder single-stage radial engines, each rated at 1,425 horsepower. This gave the aircraft a top speed of 238 mph at sea level, and a cruising speed of 150 mph. It had a service ceiling of 24,800 feet, and its range was 2,680 miles.

SA-16s were used extensively during the Korean War for search and rescue operations. Throughout the next two decades, they were assigned to Air Force units at home, in Europe, and in the Far East. In a dramatic 1954 rescue, an Albatross based at Clark AB in the Philippines was used to rescue survivors from an airliner that was shot down by Chinese fighters.

In 1950, kits were produced to retrofit 154 SA-16As as "triphibians," or aircraft that could operate from land, water or snow. These ski-equipped Albatrosses were then assigned to duty in Alaska and Greenland, where the Air Force had extensive year-round flight operations during the 1950s.

RIGHT: **US NAVY UF-1**S IN HIGH VISIBILITY LIVERY. *BELOW:* **A** COMMERCIAL **ALBATROSS** OF **CHALKS INTERNATIONAL AIRLINE.** *OPPOSITE BOTTOM:* **A US COAST GUARD UF-1** READY FOR TAKE-OFF.

In April 1955, the Air Rescue Service of the US Air Force requested a larger, longer-range Albatross. The result was the G-111. This aircraft first flew on January 16, 1956 under the designation SA-16B, but this was changed in 1962 to the search utility designation HU-16B.

The HU-16B was 62 feet 10 inches in length, 25 feet 10 inches high, and had a wing span of 96 feet 8 inches. The total wing area measured 1,035 square feet. It weighed 22,883 pounds empty, and had a gross weight of 33,000 pounds. In 1963, an Albatross set several payload records, including lifting 11,023 pounds to 19,747 feet. The HU-16B had a top speed of 236 mph at sea level, and a cruising speed of 171 mph. It had a service ceiling of 23,500 feet, and its range was 3,465 miles.

Initially, the HU-16Bs were conversions from SA-16As, but over 100 new aircraft were built. The HU-16B was also adapted for anti-submarine warfare and fitted with the AN/APS-88 search radar. For this mission, the Albatross carried a variety of armament, including Mk.43 homing torpedoes and Mk.54 depth charges.

During the Vietnam War, HU-16Bs conducted many daring search and rescue missions into enemy territory from Da Nang AB until they were replaced by helicopters in 1967. Beginning in 1955, the US Department of Interior also used a fleet of Albatrosses to provide air transportation within the Pacific Trust Territory, including the Caroline, Mariana and Marshall Islands. These aircraft were later operated under contract by Pan American Airways until 1968, when scheduled seaplane operations in the area were suspended.

Exports of Albatrosses included sales to Latin American as well as NATO countries and Japan. Many aircraft were also transferred by the US Air Force and Navy. Commercial Albatross operators included Chalks International in the Caribbean, which had operated the earlier Grumman amphibians.

RIGHT: ONE OF 10 ALBATROSSES OPERATED BY THE CANADIAN ARMED FORCES FROM 1960 TO 1971. BELOW: THIS AIR FORCE SA-16A IS PRESERVED AT THE CASTLE AIR MUSEUM IN CALIFORNIA. OPPOSITE: A US AIR FORCE HU-16B.

THE SHIN MEIWA PS-1

Shin Meiwa, which was known as Kawanishi until 1949, has perhaps the richest flying boat heritage of any company in the world that is still building seaplanes. Indeed, the best Japanese military seaplanes of World War II were Kawanishi products.

After the war, however, the company relied on maintenance work rather than new aircraft development for two decades, until 1966, when the Japanese government contracted with Shin Meiwa to build a new anti-submarine flying boat to replace the Martin Marlins then in service. The result was the SS-2 (designated as PS-1 by the Japanese Marine Self Defense Force), a four-engine aircraft whose hull and tail were quite similar to the Marlin. The PS-1 first flew on October 5, 1967, and 22 production aircraft were delivered by 1979.

In the meantime, the Japanese government ordered an amphibious variant for air-sea rescue operations under the designation US-1. This aircraft made its first flight on October 16, 1974, and deliveries began in 1975.

Both the PS-1 and US-1 are 109 feet 9.25 inches in length, 32 feet 7.75 inches high, and have a wing span of 108 feet 9 inches. The total wing area is 1,462 square feet. The aircraft weigh 56,218 pounds empty, and have a gross take-off weight of 94,800 pounds from the water, and the amphibious US-1 has a gross take-off weight from land of 99,200 pounds.

The PS-1 and US-1 are each powered by four Ishikawajima-built General Electric T64-IHI-10 turboprop engines, each rated at 3,060 horsepower.

While the PS-1 has a top speed of 340 mph, and its range is 1,347 miles, the US-1 has a top speed of 318 mph (US-1A), and a cruising speed of 265 mph at 10,000 feet. The US-1 has a service ceiling of 21,400 feet, and its range is 2,614 miles.

The PS-1 carries 20 sonobuoys and is armed with four 330-pound anti-submarine bombs, wingtip-mounted rocket launchers, and underwing pods between the engine nacelles each contain a pair of homing torpedoes. The US-1 has accommodations for a crew of nine, plus 20 seated survivors or 12 stretchers.

RIGHT: **THE PS-1** WAS BASED ON THE **SHIN MEIWA UF-XS** RESEARCH PLANE, A **GRUMMAN ALBATROSS** HEAVILY MODIFIED IN 1962. *BELOW AND OPPOSITE BOTTOM:* **THE PS-1,** SEEN HERE, RIDES ON LAND WITH RETRACTABLE BEACHING GEAR, BUT THE **US-1** HAS TRUE LANDING GEAR.

THE CANADAIR CL-215

The Canadair CL-215 amphibious flying boat was originally designed in the 1960s in response to demands from some Canadian forestry officials who were looking for a more effective way of delivering water to suppress forest fires. The aircraft was equipped with an internal, 1,410-gallon water tank system and the ability to reload its tanks in flight through two low-drag water scoops by skimming the surface of a nearby water source such as a lake or river.

The CL-215 was designed around the Pratt & Whitney R-2800 radial engines which could, at the time, be found in great abundance and at low cost. The first delivery was in 1969, and 125 CL-215 aircraft were built in five production series through 1989. These were delivered to customers in nine countries on four continents: 49 to Canada, 30 to Spain, 16 to Greece and 15 to France.

In 1987, following market trends towards more efficient, powerful and reliable turboprop engines, Canadair undertook the task of retrofitting a number of CL-215 airframes with the Pratt & Whitney Canada PW123AF engine, the same type of engine found on de Havilland and ATR regional turboprop aircraft. This retrofit aircraft was designated CL-215T and featured many aerodynamic and systems improvements as well as a 15% power increase. Powered flight controls, cockpit air conditioning, and upgraded electrical and avionics systems were incorporated. The most notable external features of the CL-215T retrofit, aside from the engines, were the aerodynamic additions to the wings and empennage.

The CL-215T gained notoriety in Southern California during the fall fire seasons of 1994 and 1995 while on lease to the Los Angeles County Fire Department for operational evaluation. The two aircraft, leased from the Province of Québec for 60 days, demonstrated their quick dispatch capability and performed repeated drops on fires in the urban-wildland interface areas of the County. In addition, the CL-215Ts demonstrated their ability to scoop water from various lakes and reservoirs as well as from the Pacific Ocean.

The CL-215 is 65 feet 0.5 inch in length, 29 feet 5.5 inches high, and has a wing span of 93 feet 10 inches. The total wing area measures 1,080 square feet. It weighs 27,938 pounds empty, and has a gross weight in water-bomber configuration of 43,500 pounds. The CL-215 was originally powered by a pair of Pratt & Whitney R-2800-CA3 18-cylinder radial engines, each rated at 2,100 horsepower and driving Hamilton Standard Hydromatic constant speed, fully-feathering, three-blade propellers. The CL-215 has a cruising speed of 188 mph, a maximum service ceiling of 20,000 feet, a range of 2,021 miles, and an endurance of 11 hours.

RIGHT: **A SPANISH CL-215** SCOOPING WATER. *BELOW:* **A CL-215** PULLS UP SHARPLY AS IT RELEASES 1,410 GALLONS OF WATER ON A FOREST FIRE. *OPPOSITE BOTTOM:* **A CL-215** COMES IN FOR A SCOOPFUL, WHILE ANOTHER LIFTS OFF WITH A LOAD.

THE CANADAIR CL-415

Canadair had 25 years of experience with the CL-215 amphibious fire-fighting aircraft when the Canadian planemaker launched the CL-415 program in 1991. The CL-415 amphibian would be a high-wing, turboprop aircraft derived from the CL-215 and featuring a four-compartment, four-door water tank system that could hold 1,622 gallons of water or a water/foam mixture. Like its predecessor, the CL-415 refills its tanks by skimming the surface of any suitable body of water.

Although it is externally similar to its predecessor, the CL-415 is essentially a new aircraft. It features Pratt & Whitney Canada turboprops, an air-conditioned glass cockpit, and powered flight controls. Compared to the CL-215,

it has increased operating weight and speed, yielding improved performance and productivity. The CL-415 is 65 feet 0.5 inch in length, 29 feet 5.5 inches high, and has a wing span of 93 feet 11 inches. It weighs 28,353 pounds empty, has a take-off weight of 43,850 pounds and a maximum after-scooping weight of 46,000 pounds. The CL-415 is powered by a pair of Pratt & Whitney PW123AF turboprop engines, each rated at up to 2,380 shaft horsepower.

The CL-415 has a top speed of 226 mph, a rate of climb of 1,375 feet per second, and its range is 1,500 miles. Its maximum scooping distance is 3,900 feet and the

RIGHT AND BELOW: A GOVERNMENT OF QUÉBEC CL-415 SCOOPING WATER. OPPOSITE BOTTOM: THE PILOT BRAVES DENSE SMOKE AND LEAPING FLAMES, RELEASES HIS LOAD OF FIRE RETARDANT AND PULLS UP FAST.

tanks can be filled in 12 seconds. The CL-415 picks up water through two small scoops only 3 x 5 inches in cross section. These are lowered into the water when the airplane touches down to refill its tanks.

In its firefighting configuration, the CL-415 is geared toward "initial attack" on forest fires, i.e. in getting to the fire at the earliest stages and dropping large amounts of fire suppressing water and foam with great frequency.

The CL-415 production program was launched in October 1991 with an initial order of 12 aircraft for France and eight for the government of Québec. In 1994, Italy ordered four CL-415s, followed by two more in March

1996. The CL-415 first flew in December 1993 and the first aircraft was delivered in November 1994.

Subsequently, Canadair (now a Division of Bombardier, Incorporated) proposed the CL-415M, a multi-role derivative for surveillance, military applications or emergency services. With its amphibious capabilities, the CL-415M was seen as applicable for parts of the world where there are long coastlines or many islands to survey.

The CL-415M was developed to feature mission sensors such as a surveillance radar and FLIR (forward-looking infrared) as well as precision navigation and high-power communications equipment.

RIGHT: THE **CL-415M,** SEEN HERE IN AIR-SEA RESCUE CONFIGURATION, IS A MULTI-ROLE VARIANT OF THE TURBO-PROP FIRE-BOMBER. *BELOW:* AS AVIATION ENTERS ITS SECOND CENTURY, THE **CL-415** IS ONE OF THE MOST IMPORTANT FLYING BOATS IN PRODUCTION IN THE WORLD.

INDEX

Adriatic Sea 38
Ady, Howard 95
Aegean Sea 103
Aerial Experiment Association 10
Aero Club of America's Expert
    Aviator Certificate 16
Aero Espresso 22, 60
Afrika Korps 130
Air France 52, 98
Aircraft Scouting Force 100
Ala Littoria 60
Alexandria 64
Allison J71-A-6 140
Allison J75-P-2 142
Allison T40-A-10 146
Allison XT40-A-4 144
American Airways 78
American Export Airlines 98
American Museum of Natural
    History 93-94
America 10
Amphibians 8, 48, 51, 152, 154,
    156, 162, 164, 168, 170
Amsterdam 60
Amundsen, Roald 47
Anacostia, Virginia 18, 28
Angmagssalik, Greenland 75
Ansett Australian 122
Antilles Air Boats 122
Arado Ar.95 102
Arado Ar.195 102
Arado Ar.196 102-103
Archbold, Richard, Dr. 93-94
Areoservices Parrague 98
Argentina 36, 54
Argentine Navy 70
Armistice Day 24
Art deco 6
Atlantic Ocean 6, 8, 10, 18, 30,
    44, 47, 64-65, 75, 108, 112, 130,
    136
Auriol, Jacqueline 154
Australia 64, 128, 152
Aviolanda 104, 106
Azores 10, 60

B&W (Boeing Model 1) 12-13
Bacula, Adriano 40
Bahamasair 98
Baird, Henri 38
Balbo, Italo 58-60
Barcelona 45
Bay of Biscay 103, 132
Beech 18 7
Bel Geddes, Norman 44
Bell, Alexander Graham 10
Bennett, Floyd 78
Beriev A40 Albatross 7
Bethpage, Long Island 154
Biesel, Rex 128
Bishop, Lillian Fleet 28
Bismarck 95, 102-103
Black Sea 103
Blohm und Voss Bv.138 112-113

Blohm und Voss Bv.222 Wiking
    130-133
BMW 132K 91, 103
BMW IV 46
BMW-Bramo 323R-2 106, 107,
    132
Boeing Airplane Company 12, 18-
    19, 28, 70, 80, 92
Boeing, William Edward "Bill" 12,
    70-71
Boeing 247 78
Boeing 314 Clipper 84-89
Boeing B-1 20-21
Boeing B-15 84
Boeing B-17 84
Boeing B-29 84
Boeing C-5 floatplanes 13
Boeing Clippers 86
Bombardier, Incorporated 172
Boothman, John 42
Brazil 36, 47, 154
Bristol Hercules 637 122
Bristol IV Hercules 64
Bristol Jupiter VIII 47
Bristol Jupiter 45
Bristol Pegasus VI 76
Bristol Pegasus XC 64, 67
Bristol Pegasus XVIII 120
Bristol Pegasus XXII 119
Bristol Perseus XIIc 64
Britain 8, 34, 38, 40-41, 47, 64,
    91-92, 95, 118, 128, 152
Britain, Battle of 42
British Empire 64
British Imperial Airways 64, 66-67
British Overseas Airways Company
    (BOAC) 64, 86, 122
Brow, Harold 40
Browning machine gun 36, 94
Buenos Aires 72
Buffalo, New York 28, 54, 92
Bureau of Aeronautics 40
Byrd, Richard Evelyn 78

Cadiz 45
Cagno, Stefano 58
Calypso 64, 98
Campinelli, Ernesto 22-23
Canadair (company) 8
Canadair CL-215 168-170
Canadair CL-415 170-171
Canopus 64-65
Cant 6ter 22
Cant 10ter 23
Cantieri Cavali Triestini (CANT)
    22, 23
Cape Cod 18
Cape Town, South Africa 67
Caribbean 30, 62, 72, 86, 98,
    152, 164
Castle Air Museum 165
Catalina Air Lines 153
Catalina Channel Air Service 71
Catalina Island 16

Cathay Pacific 98
Centurion 64
Cessna 8
Chalks International Airline 156,
    163-164
Chase, William 95
Chesapeake Bay 40
Chiang Kai-shek 36
Chicago World's Fair 60
Chile 98, 128
China Clipper 81-83
China National Aviation 71
Churchill, Winston 86
Clark Air Base 162
Cleveland 27
Clio 64
Clippers 6, 72-73, 80-89
Clover Field 48
Coco Solo Naval Air Station 18,
    54
Colombia 54
Congo River 94
Congressional Medal of Honor 36
Consolidated (company) 32, 54,
    116, 135
Consolidated B-36 45
Consolidated Commodore 28, 30-
    31, 54
Consolidated OA-10 96
Consolidated P2Y Ranger 54-57,
    92
Consolidated PB2Y Coronado
    100-101, 144
Consolidated PBY Catalina 9, 92-
    99, 144
Consolidated PY series 28-29, 32,
    54
Consolidated Vultee Aircraft Corp-
    oration (see Convair)
Consolidated XPY-1 Admiral 28-
    30
Constantine 60
Construzzioni Meccaniche Aero-
    nautiche 46
Convair (company) 140
Convair F-102 150
Convair F2Y (see Convair
    SeaDart)
Convair P5Y/R3Y Tradewind 144-
    147
Convair SeaDart 150-151
Coral Sea Tradewind 146
Cousteau, Jacques 98-99
Crimea 106
Cuba 36
Cuddihy, George 40
Culver City, California 148
Curtiss, Glenn Hammond 6, 10-
    11, 16, 92, 138
Curtiss (company) 12, 24, 28
Curtiss C-1 9
Curtiss CD12 38
Curtiss Condor 78-79
Curtiss Conqueror V-12 45

Curtiss CR 38
Curtiss D Hydro 10-11
Curtiss F2C 38
Curtiss F3C 38
Curtiss H-1 *America* 11, 18
Curtiss HS series 18-19
Curtiss *June Bug* 10
Curtiss NC-4 10
Curtiss O3C 48
Curtiss OX-5 12
Curtiss R2C 38, 40
Curtiss R3C series 38, 40
Curtiss R4C 78
Curtiss T32 Condor 78-79
Curtiss Type O 10
Curtiss V-1400 40
Curtiss VXX 18

Da Nang Air Base 164
Daimler-Benz DB.603V 1 132
Daimler-Benz GmbH 158
Dakar 52, 94
Darden, Colgate III 71
Dark Head Cove 25
deHavilland Aircraft 160, 168
deHavilland Beaver series 6, 8,
    160-161
de Pinedo, Francesco 22-23, 58
De Schelde 104, 106
del Prete, Carlo 58
Denmark 90, 112
Detroit & Cleveland Navigation
    Company 30
Deutsche Luft Hansa (later
    Lufthansa) 47, 108-109, 111, 130
di Bernardi, Mario 40
Dismore, S.A. 64
Disney, Walt 96
Dixie Clipper 85-86
DNL 122
Dominican Republic 128
Doolittle, Jimmy 40
Dornier (company) 8, 52
Dornier, Claudius 44-46, 158
Dornier Do.24 series 104-108,
    112, 158-159
Dornier Do.26 108-112
Dornier Do.J Wal (Whale) 44, 46-
    47, 104, 108
Dornier Do.L Delphin (Dolphin)
    46, 69-71
Dornier Do.R Super Wal 47
Dornier Do.X 44-45, 52, 84, 104
Dornier GmbH 158
Dornier Seastar 158-159
Douglas Aircraft Company 48, 68
Douglas, Donald 48, 68
Douglas Cloudster 48
Douglas DC-1 68
Douglas DC-series monoplanes 78
Douglas Dolphin series 68-71
Douglas DT series 48
Douglas O2D 48, 51
Douglas OA-3 70

Douglas OA-4 70
Douglas PD-1 48
Douglas T2D 48
Douglas World Cruisers 48
Douglas XO2D 48-51
Dundee, Scotland 67, 90
Duralumin 47
Duramold 148

East Greenwich, Rhode Island 28
East Indies 96, 106
Easter Island 98
Eastern Air Transport 78
Elliot Bay 85
Elsworth, Lincoln 47
Emperor Bao Dai 154
Empire Airmail Scheme 64
English Channel 91
Esders, Armand 70
Evergreen Adventure Museum
    148

Fabre, Henri 6, 10
Felixstowe (company) 18
Felixstowe F.2 10
Fiat (company) 47
Fiat A.24R 60
Fiat AS.2 40
Fire-fighting aircraft 168-172
Fleet, Reuben 28, 30, 54, 62, 92
FLIR (forward-looking infrared)
    172
Flitestar Angkasa 158
Floatplanes 6, 8, 12, 14, 37, 102,
    138
Flying boats 6, 8, 22-24, 28, 32,
    35, 44-46, 52, 58, 66, 84, 92, 112,
    116, 118, 130, 138, 140, 144, 166,
    168, 173
Flying Calypso 98-99
Flying Tankers Limited 124, 126
Focke-Wulf Fw.62 102
France 34, 47, 52, 95, 112, 132,
    154, 168, 172
Friedrichshafen 45

Gallaudet 18, 28
Gallipoli, Battle of 15
General Electric T64-IHI-10 166
Gennariello 22
Genoa 22, 45
Germany 8, 46, 90, 104, 106
Gibraltar 45, 60, 64
Gilles, Bud 154
Gloster IIA 40
Gloster IV biplanes 42
Golden Gate Bridge 83
Gorton, A.W. 28
Great Depression 30, 45, 68
Greece 106
Greenland 74, 78, 162
Grumman Aircraft Corporation
    114
Grumman, Leroy 114

Grumman, Roy 154
Grumman Albatross series 162-165, 167
Grumman Duck series 114-115, 154
Grumman F-14 Tomcat 114
Grumman F4F Wildcat 114
Grumman F6F Hellcat 114
Grumman F8F Bearcat 114
Grumman F9F Cougar 147
Grumman F9F Panther 114
Grumman Goose series 152-154, 156, 162
Grumman Gosling Mk.I 154
Grumman HU-16 164-165
Grumman Mallard series 156-157
Grumman OA-14 154
Grumman OA-9 152
Grumman UC4F 154
Grumman UF 162-163
Grumman Widgeon series 154-155
Guam 82
Guba 93-94
Guidoni, Alessandro 45
Gulf War 114

Haifa 60
Haiti 36
Hall, Charles Martin 28
Hall XPH-1 29
Hall-Aluminum Company 28
Hall-Scott A-5 12
Hall-Scott A-7A 12
Hall-Scott L-6 20
Hamburger Flugzeugwerke 112-113
Hamburg 159
Hammondsport, New York 10
Hampton Roads, Virginia 18, 40
Hawaii 62
Hawaii Clipper 82
Heinkel, Ernst, Flugzeug Werke 90
Heinkel He.115 series 90-91
Heinkel He.162 90
Heinkel He.177/277 90
Heinkel He.219 90
Helicopters 8, 138, 164
Hispano-Suiza (company) 47
Hispano-Suiza 12N 52
Hispano-Suiza 12Y 52
Hitler, Adolf 112
HMS *Ben-My-Chree* 14
HMS *Pegasus* 129
Hollandia, New Guinea 94
Hong Kong 82
Hubbard, Eddie 12, 21
Hughes, Howard Robard 44, 148
Hughes HK-1 "Spruce Goose" 44, 124, 148-149
Hydroplanes 6, 10, 92

Iceland 60
Imperial Russia 62
India 64

Indian Ocean 94, 118
Indian Ocean Tradewind 146
Indonesia 94, 104
Inshore Patrol 128
Inter-Island Airways 62
Inuit people 74
Ireland 60
Irvine, Rutledge 38
Isle of Wight 38
Isotta-Fraschini 22-23
Isotta-Fraschini Semi-Asso 34, 61
Italy 8, 22-23, 34, 38, 40, 46-47, 104, 150, 172
Iwo Jima 100

Japan 8, 36, 47, 54, 116, 164
Johnson, Martin 62
Johnson, Osa 62
Junkers Jumo 205D 108
Junkers W.33 36
Jutland, Battle of 15

Kaiser, Henry J. 148
Kawanishi (company) 166
Kawanishi H6K 54
Kawanishi H8K 116-117
Key West 18
King Farouk 156
Klemusch, Oberleutnant Wolfgang 112
KLM (Royal Dutch Airlines) 98
Korean War 156, 162
Kriegsmarine (German Navy) 102-103, 112

Lac Berre 6
Laddon, I.M. "Mac" 28, 30, 54, 92
Lake Constance 45
Lake Erie 28, 30
Lake Habbema 93-94
Lake Keuka 10-11
Lake Union 12-13
Lake Victoria 94
Lancaster bomber 132
Latécoère (company) 52
Latécoère 300 52-53
Latécoère 521 52
Latécoère *Croix du Sud* 52-53
Levanesky, Sigismund 94
Liberty 12 engine 18, 20
Liberty Island 31
Lindbergh, Anne Morrow 74-75
Lindbergh, Charles 62, 72, 74-75
Lisbon 86, 108
Lockheed Model 8 Sirius 74
Lockheed Sirius *Tingmissartoq* 74-75
Lohner flying boat 34
Long Beach Harbor 148-149
Loon 10
Lorraine 47
Lorraine-Dietrich 22-23
Los Angeles 48

Los Angeles County Fire Department 168
Loughead (later Lockheed) 18
Lufthansa (see Deutsche Luft Hansa)
Luftwaffe 90-91, 106-109, 111-113, 130
Lycoming GO-435-C2B 154
Lycoming GO-480-B1D 154

MacArthur, Douglas, General 95
Macchi (company) 6, 150
Macchi M.33 40
Macchi M.39 39, 40, 42
Macchi M.5 34-35, 150
Macchi M.52 40
Macchi M.67 42
Macchi M.7 34-35, 38
Macchi M.9 35
Maddalena, Umberto 45, 58
Magnetic anomaly detection 139
Maia 67
Malta 91
Manila 82
Manila Harbor 73
Marchetti, Alessandro 58
Marianas Mars 126
Marine Luchtvaartdienst 104
Mariner GR.I 136
Marseilles 45, 52, 86
Marshall Islands 116
Martigues 6
Martin (company) 16, 28, 32, 84, 134
Martin, Glenn Luther 16
Martin M-130 Clipper 80-84
Martin Mariner series 134-137
Martin Marlin series 138-139, 144, 166
Martin Mars series 124-127, 132, 146, 148
Martin MO-1 16-17
Martin Model 63 26
Martin Model R 16
Martin Model S 16-17
Martin Model TA Hydro 16
Martin MS-1 26-27
Martin P3M 28, 32-33, 54
Martin P5M Marlin 138-139, 144, 146
Martin P6M SeaMaster 140-143
Martin PBM Mariner 134-137
Martin PM series 24-25
Martin TT 16-17
Martin XP2M 32-33
Mathis 8G40 154
Mayo, R.H. 66-67
McGinnis, Knefler 54
McKinnon Enterprises 152, 154
McKinnon Super Widgeon 154
McKinnon-Viking 152
Mediterranean 60, 64, 76, 103, 112, 131
Melbourne 22
Mercury 67
Mexican air corps 30

Mexico 36, 128
Miami 18
Middle River, Maryland 143
Midway Island 81, 82
Midway, Battle of 95-96
Mitchell, Reginald J. 40-42, 76
Mitsubishi Kasai 22 116
Mitsubishi "Zero" 116
Monaco 38
Montreal 60, 92
Moscow 75, 112
Motu people 94
Musick, Ed 72-73

Nakajima 36
Napier Lion VIIB 40
Napier Rapier V16 66
Natal, Brazil 47, 52-53
National Geographic Magazine 30
National Security Act 162
NATO 164
Naval Air Station Banana River 137
Naval Air Station North Island 11, 17, 138
Naval Air Transport Service 134
Naval Aircraft Factory 18, 24, 36, 92
Navy Sesquicentennial Exposition 27
Netherlands 46, 104-106
Netherlands East Indies 93-94, 152
Netherlands Marine Luchtvaart-dienst (Naval Air Ministry) 104
New York 45, 60, 72, 75, 86, 108
New York, Rio & Buenos Aires (NYRBA) 30, 62
New Zealand 12
Newfoundland 10
Newman, George 100
Newport Bay 16
Nicaragua 36
Nieuport (company) 34
Nobile, Umberto 58
Norfolk Navy Yard 40, 54
North Pole 47, 78
North Sea 90-91, 112-113
North to the Orient 74
Northrop (company) 114
Northrop, Jack 74
Norway 47, 90-91, 106, 108-109, 112, 130
NYRBA Commodore *Havana* 31

Offerdahl, Haakon 91
O'Neill, Ralph, Captain 30
Orbatello 58
Osa's Ark 62

Pacific Ocean 6, 8, 30, 72, 74, 81-82, 96, 116-118, 124-126, 136, 146, 168
Pacific Rim 80

Pacific Trust Territory 164
Pan American Airways 30, 62-63, 71-72, 80, 84-86, 154, 164
Pan American Clippers 6, 72-73, 80-89
Panama Canal Zone 54
Panama 62
Paris 75
Pavia 23
Pearl Harbor 94-95, 116
Pelican (see Grumman Albatross)
Penang 158
Peru 36
Philadelphia 27, 92
Philippines 100, 162
Philippine Clipper 81-82
Philippine Mars 126
Piaggio P.166 7
Pisa, Italy 46
Point Loma, California 146
Polar Cat 99
Pontoons 12, 38, 48, 51, 54, 78
Portugal 45, 154
Pratt &Whiney Hornet 30, 72
Pratt &Whitney PW123AF 170
Pratt &Whitney R-985 series 128, 152
Pratt &Whitney R-1340 series 28, 32, 36, 48, 74
Pratt &Whitney R-1690 32
Pratt &Whitney R-1830 series 80, 98, 100
Pratt &Whitney R-2800 series 136, 168
Pratt &Whitney R-4360 124, 148
Pratt &Whitney Twin Wasp series 36, 62, 119, 120, 122
Pratt & Whitney Wasp S3H1 156
Pratt &Whitney Canada PT6A series 152, 158, 160
Pratt &Whitney Canada PT6D-6 160
Pratt & Whitney Canada PW123AF 168
Project Baker 101
Pulitzer race 38, 40
Pullman service 82

Qantas 64, 98
Québec 168, 171-172

Rand, James H. 30
Ranger 6-440C-5 154
Regia Aeronautica (Italian Air Force) 58-60
Reichsluftfahrtministerium (German Air Ministry) 90
Remington Rand 30
Richards, W. L. 95
Richbourg, Chuck 150
Rio de Janiero 58
Rittenhouse, David 38
Roaring twenties 45, 68
Rohr Aircraft 100
Rolls Royce Eagle IX 47

Rolls Royce V 42
Rome 22, 60
Roosevelt, Franklin 70, 86
Ross Sound 79
Royal Air Force 40, 42, 64, 67,
    97, 118-119, 121, 135-136
Royal Australian Air Force 106,
    121
Royal Canadian Air Force 152
Royal Navy 10, 14, 154
Russian Revolution 62

Saipan 135
Salmson 14
San Diego 10, 18, 25, 54, 92-94,
    100, 138, 144-145, 150-151
San Francisco 54, 81-83, 86
San Pedro 69
San Remo 22
SA Navigazione Aerea (SANA) 45
Santa Maria 58, 60
Santa Monica 48, 68-69
SAS (Scandinavian Air Service) 122
Saunders-Roe (company) 76
Saunders-Roe SR.A/1 150
Savoia Marchetti (company) 8,
    22-23
Savoia Marchetti S.55 58-61
Savoia S.13 38
Savoia S.16 series 22-23
Schneider Trophy Races 6, 35,
    38-43, 76
Schneider, Jacques 38
Scotland 136
Sea of Marmara 14
Seattle 12, 19-21, 70, 72, 84-85
Seeadler (Sea Eagle) 108-109
Seine River 154
Senegal 52
Sepik River 96
Sesto Calende, Lake Maggiore 22
Shanghai 36
Shannon, Sam 144
Shin Meiwa (company) 8
Shin Meiwa PS-1 166-167

Shin Meiwa SS-2 166
Shin Meiwa UF-XS 167
Shin Meiwa US-1 166-167
Short Brothers 8, 64, 118, 122
Short, Eustace 14
Short, Horace 14
Short 74 14
Short 166 15
Short 184 14-15
Short Folder 14
Short G.26 Golden Hind 65
Short Mk.I 119
Short Mk.II 119-121
Short Mk.III 119
Short Mk.V 118, 120
Short S.23 Empire 64, 66, 118,
    122
Short S.25 Sunderland 118-122
Short S.25V Sandringham 122-
    123
Short S.45 Solent 122
Short Seaford 122
Short/Mayo Composite 66-67
Short/Mayo S.20 Mercury 66
Short/Mayo S.21 Maia 66
Sikorsky (company) 84
Sikorsky, Igor 62, 72
Sikorsky S-32 62
Sikorsky S-34 62
Sikorsky S-38 62-63
Sikorsky S-40 72, 80
Sikorsky S-42 Clipper 72-73, 80
Sinbad (see Douglas Dolphin)
Singapore 64
Societa Aerea Mediterranea 60
Societa Anonima Macchi 34
Societa Idrovolanti Alta Italia (see
    Savoia)
Societa Italiana Servizi Aerei 22-
    23
Société de Constructions Aéro-
    navales 154
South Pacific 98
South Pole 79
Southampton 42

Southern Cross (see Latécoère
    Croix du Sud)
Soviet Air Force 7
Soviet Union 92, 112
Spain 46, 106, 168
Spruce Goose 44, 124, 148-149
St. Louis 40
St. Thomas 94
Standard Oil Company 70
Stout, Ernest 144
Strawberry Point Hangar 141
Sunbeam 15
Super Cat 99
Supermarine (company) 6, 38
Supermarine S.4 40
Supermarine S.5 40-41
Supermarine S.6 42-43
Supermarine Seagull 76
Supermarine Spitfire 42, 76
Supermarine Walrus 76-77
Sweden 47, 90
Sydney, Australia 94

Tanner, William P. 95
Thai Airways 98
Thailand 154
Thunderbird Air 161
Tiber River 22
Tokyo 22
Titan II ICBM (Martin) 142
Titan III (Martin) 142
Trans-Australian 98
Treasure Island 81
Treaty of Versailles 46, 104
Trieste 23, 45
Triphibians 162
Trippe, Juan 80
Turin 23

U-boats 96, 103, 112, 118, 120,
    128, 148, 154
Uruguay 128
US Air Force 160, 162, 164, 165
US Antarctic Service 78
US Army 12, 16, 38, 48, 70, 78,

40, 79
US Army Air Corps 28, 69, 152
US Coast Guard 68, 71-69, 114,
    154, 162-163
US Department of Interior 164
US Marine Corps 36, 78, 68, 71,
    144
US Naval Aircraft Factory 18 24, 36, 92
US Navy 9-10, 12, 16, 18, 24, 26,
    28, 30, 32, 36-38, 40, 48, 51, 54-
    55, 68, 71, 78-79, 86, 92, 94-95,
    97-100, 114-115, 124, 126, 128,
    134, 136, 138, 140, 142, 144, 146,
    150, 152, 154, 162-164
US Navy Bureau of Aeronautics
    40
USS Colorado 128
USS Grayback 26
USS Growler 26
USS Halibut 26
USS Langley 26
USS Maryland 36
USS Mississippi 17
USS Pennsylvania 10
USS Raleigh 37
USS Ward 95

Vancouver, British Columbia 12
Vanderbilt family 70
Venezuela 152
Venice 23, 38, 40, 45
Vickers K machine gun 76
Vickers/Canadair 92
Victoria, British Columbia 20-21
Vietnam 138, 154
Vietnam War 164
Vogt, Richard 130
Vought, Chance 36
Vought O2U Corsair 36-37
Vought O5U 48
Vought OS2U Kingfisher 9, 128-
    129
Vought Regulus SSM-N cruise mis-
    sile 26
Vought UO 36

Vought VE-7 36-37

Waghorn, H.R.D. 42-43
Wake Island 82
Water-scoopers 8, 168-173
Webster, S.N. 42
West Indies 94
Westervelt, Conrad 12
Westinghouse J46-WE-12B 150
Wheatly, Bill 92, 100
Wilkins, Hubert, Sir 94
Williams, Alford 40
Wilmington-Catalina Airlines 71
World Airways 86
World War I 10, 12, 14, 16, 18,
    20, 32, 34, 38, 44, 46, 76, 150
World War II 8, 26, 28, 40, 42,
    44, 46, 52, 54, 64, 67, 82, 84, 86,
    90, 92, 95, 98, 108, 112, 114, 116,
    118, 124, 128, 130, 132, 134, 138,
    148, 150, 152-154, 156, 162, 166
World's Fair 94
Worsley, O.E. 42
Wright Cyclone 79, 106
Wright GR-2600 84
Wright R-1820 series 24, 32, 54,
    104, 114, 162
Wright R-2600-22 134
Wright R-3350 series 124, 138
Wright SR-1839 74
Wright, Orville 10
Wright, Wilbur 10
Wright-Martin 16

Yamal Peninsula 112
Yankee Clipper 84, 86

Zeppelin-Werke GmbH 44, 46

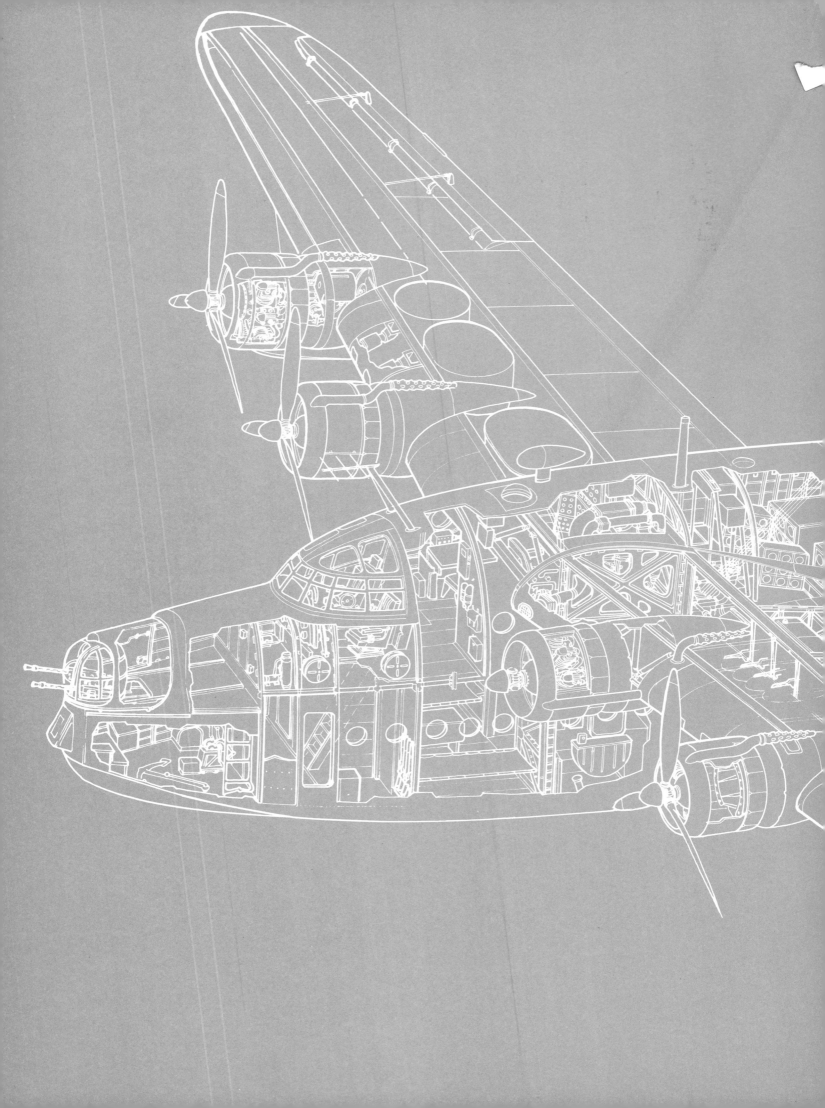